United Nations Conference on Trade and Development

Investment Policy Review
El Salvador

UNITED NATIONS
New York and Geneva, 2010

NOTE

UNCTAD serves as the focal point within the United Nations Secretariat for all matters related to foreign direct investment, as part of its work on trade and development. This function was formerly carried out by the United Nations Centre on Transnational Corporations (1975–1992). UNCTAD's work is carried out through intergovernmental deliberations, research and analysis, technical assistance activities, seminars, workshops and conferences.

The term "country" as used in this study also refers, as appropriate, to territories or areas; the designations employed and the presentation of the material do not imply the expression of any opinion whatsoever on the part of the Secretariat of the United Nations concerning the legal status of any country, territory, city or area or of its authorities, or concerning the delimitation of its frontiers or boundaries. In addition, the designations of country groups are intended solely for statistical or analytical convenience and do not necessarily express a judgment about the stage of development reached by a particular country or area in the development process.

The following symbols have been used in the tables:

Two dots (..) indicate that data are not available or not separately reported. Rows in tables have been omitted in those cases where no data are available for any of the elements in the row.

A hyphen (-) indicates that the item is equal to zero or its value is negligible.

A blank in a table indicates that the item is not applicable.

A slash (/) between dates representing years – for example, 2007/08, indicates a financial year.

The use of a dash (–) between dates representing years, for example 2007–2008, signifies the full period involved, including the beginning and end years.

Reference to dollars ($) means United States dollars, unless otherwise indicated.

Annual rates of growth or change, unless otherwise stated, refer to annual compound rates.

Details and percentages in tables do not necessarily add up to the totals because of rounding.

The material contained in this study may be freely quoted with appropriate acknowledgement.

UNCTAD/DIAE/PCB/2009/20

UNITED NATIONS PUBLICATION
Sales number E.10.II.D.15
ISBN 978-92-1-112797-3

PREFACE

The UNCTAD *Investment Policy Reviews* are intended to help countries improve their investment policies and to familiarize governments and the international private sector with an individual country's investment environment. The reviews are considered by the UNCTAD Commission on Investment, Enterprise and Development.

The *Investment Policy Review of El Salvador*, initiated at the request of the Salvadorean Government, was carried out by means of a fact-finding mission in May 2009, and is based on information current at that date. The mission received the full cooperation of the relevant ministries and agencies, in particular El Salvador's investment promotion agency, PROESA. The mission also had the benefit of the views of the private sector, both foreign and domestic, and of the resident international community, particularly bilateral donors and development agencies. This draft was discussed with stakeholders at a national workshop in San Salvador on 17 February 2010.

The suitability and effectiveness of the regulatory regime is assessed against several related criteria: (a) whether regulations adequately promote and protect the public interest; (b) whether regulations adequately promote investment and sustainable socio-economic development; and (c) whether the methods employed are effective and well administered, given their public interest and development objectives and the legitimate concerns of investors that rules and procedures should not unduly burden their competitiveness. International practices are taken into account in making the assessments and recommendations in this report.

This report was prepared by the Investment Policy Reviews section, under the direction of Chantal Dupasquier and the supervision of James Zhan. It was drafted by Quentin Dupriez, Rory Allan, Hans Baumgarten and Lizzie Medrano. Irina Stanyukova provided statistical assistance. The report benefited from comments and suggestions from UNCTAD colleagues, under a peer-review process. It was edited by Daniel Sanderson.

It is hoped that the analysis and recommendations in this review will help El Salvador achieve its development goals, contribute to improved policies, promote dialogue among stakeholders, and catalyse investment and the beneficial impact of foreign direct investment.

Geneva, april 2010

TABLE OF CONTENTS

TABLES

FIGURES

BOXES

ABBREVIATIONS

BCR	Banco Central de Reserva de El Salvador
BIT	bilateral investment treaty
BPO	business process outsourcing
BVES	Bolsa de Valores de El Salvador
CACM	Central American Common Market
CAFTA-DR	Central America–Dominican Republic–United States Free Trade Agreement
CAUCA	Central American Uniform Customs Code
CEL	Comisión Hidroeléctrica del Río Lempa
CNR	Centro Nacional de Registros
CONADEI	Comisión Nacional de Promoción de Exportaciones e Inversiones
CSR	corporate social responsibility
DTT	double taxation treaty
EIA	environmental impact assessment
EMPRESAL	Programa Empresa Salvadoreña para la Responsabilidad Social
EPZ	export processing zone
ESE	environmental strategy evaluation
FDI	foreign direct investment
FUNDEMAS	Fundación Empresarial para la Acción Social
FUSADES	Fundación Salvadoreña para el Desarrollo Económico y Social
GDP	gross domestic product
GFCF	gross fixed capital formation
GHG	greenhouse gases
GNI	gross national income
GSP	Generalized System of Preferences
GWh	gigawatt-hour
ICSID	International Centre for Settlement of Investment Disputes
ICT	information and communications technologies
ILO	International Labour Organization
IMF	International Monetary Fund
IPA	investment promotion agency
MARN	Ministerio de Medio Ambiente y Recursos Naturales
MDG	Millennium Development Goal
MFN	most favoured nation
MRS	Mercado Regulador del Sistema
MW	megawatt
OECD	Organization for Economic Cooperation and Development
ONI	Oficina Nacional de Inversiones

PPP	public–private partnership
PROESA	Agencia de Promoción de Inversión de El Salvador
R&D	research and development
SIGET	Superintendencia General de Electricidad y Telecomunicaciones
SINAMA	Sistema Nacional de Gestión del Medio Ambiente
SMEs	small and medium-sized enterprises
TNC	transnational corporation
TRIPS	Trade-Related Aspects of Intellectual Property Rights
UNDP	United Nations Development Programme
UNFCCC	United Nations Framework Convention on Climate Change
UT	Unidad de Transacciones
VAT	value-added tax
WCO	World Customs Organization
WEF	World Economic Forum
WTO	World Trade Organization

EL SALVADOR

Key investment climate indicators (2009)

	El Salvador	Costa Rica	Panama	CACM
Starting a business (number of days)	17.0	60.0	12.0	31.8
Cost of registering property (percentage of property value)	3.8	3.4	2.4	3.5
Investor protection index (0–10)	4.3	3.0	4.7	3.9
Employment rigidity index (0–100)	24.0	39.0	66.0	35.0
Difficulty of hiring index (0–100)	33.0	78.0	78.0	55.4
Redundancy costs (weeks of wage)	86.0	29.0	44.0	66.6
Cost enforcing contracts (% claim)	19.2	24.3	50.0	26.4
Fixed local telecommunications cost ($ per 3 minute call, peak rate)	0.1	0.0	0.1	0.1
Time for exports (days)	14.0	13.0	9.0	18.6
Time for imports (days)	10.0	15.0	9.0	18.8
Domestic investment (% GDP)	14.6	24.1	23.7	21.7

Sources: World Bank, *Doing Business;* and UNCTAD.

Key economic and social indicators

Indicator	1991–2000 average	2001–2007 average	2008	CACM 2008
Population (in millions)	5.7	6.0	6.1	37.3
GDP at market prices (in billions of dollars)	9.5	16.4	22.1	112.2
GDP per capita (dollars)	1644.6	2719.6	3605.3	3005.9
Real GDP growth (percentage)	4.6	3.0	2.5	3.3
GDP by sector (percentage):				
Agriculture	13.5	9.8	12.7	11.3
Industry	29.0	29.5	27.4	28.3
Services	57.5	60.8	59.9	60.4
Inflation (percentage)	8.4	3.6	7.3	11.7
Trade (in billions of dollars):				
Merchandise exports	1.7	3.3	4.5	26.1
Services exports	0.5	1.1	1.6	9.0
Merchandise imports	3.1	6.5	9.8	52.8
Services imports	0.6	1.2	2.1	8.2
Exports to GDP ratio	21.8	26.8	27.7	35.4
Imports to GDP ratio	35.8	44.4	49.8	55.0
Capital flows (in billions of dollars):[1]				
Net FDI flows	0.2	0.5	1.5	5.3
Net flows from private creditors	0.0	0.4	-0.1	0.1
Net flows from official creditors	0.1	0.1	0.0	0.5
Grants	0.3	0.2	0.2	4.2
FDI inflow to GDP ratio	1.4	2.9	3.6	4.6
Life expectancy at birth (years)	68.9	70.8	71.4	72.7
Infant mortality (per thousand) [1,2]	33.0	21.8	20.6	21.8
Literacy rate, adult (percentage) [1,2]	74.1	82.8	82.0	82.6
Literacy rate, youth (percentage) [1,2]	84.9	94.3	93.6	91.6

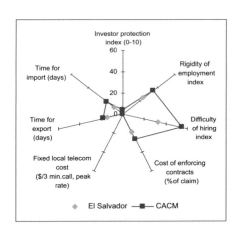

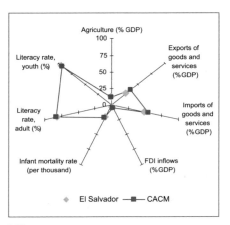

[1] The most recent data are for 2007.   [2] Averages calculated from years for which data are available.

Sources: UNCTAD, FDI/TNC database; World Bank, *World Development Indicators*; World Bank, *Global Development Finance.*

INTRODUCTION

El Salvador has long adopted an open attitude towards foreign direct investment (FDI) and it is basing its development strategy on a policy of openness to trade, investment and international competitive pressures. A large number of reforms have been implemented in the past decades, including the dollarization of the economy in 2001 and a privatization programme that includes services such as banking, electricity and telecommunications.

The strategy to develop as an open market economy and to subject local operators to international competitive pressures has yielded positive results for the country, on balance. And yet much progress remains to be made in order to eradicate poverty and reduce income inequality. In addition, El Salvador faces the challenge of further improving the competitiveness of locally established companies and increasing its attractiveness as a destination of choice for foreign companies participating in global supply chains. FDI could play a bigger catalytic role in the future, and this review offers recommendations in that regard.

Chapter I analyses past trends in FDI, and the impact of FDI on the economy. It notes that the country has come a long way in transforming its economy and in developing the industrial and services sectors. In addition, El Salvador has managed to develop a quality road, electricity and telecommunications infrastructure. Ports and human capital, however, remain weak. Well-managed reforms have enabled El Salvador to successfully attract FDI in infrastructure, including telecommunications and electricity. Banking has also been a key magnet for foreign investors, and FDI in export-processing zones has helped boost exports and create employment. Foreign investors have also been active in niche sectors. Larger and more diversified FDI inflows are achievable, however, and foreign investors could contribute further to the development of a competitive open economy.

Chapter II examines the investment framework. It notes that El Salvador made a firm strategic choice to develop as an open market economy decades ago, and that this is reflected strongly in the regulatory framework. It commends El Salvador for the progress it has achieved, not only in establishing the laws and regulations needed to operate a market economy fairly, efficiently and in accordance with development goals, but also in putting into place strong regulatory institutions. It offers recommendations on key areas where further improvement is needed, including corporate taxation, customs, environmental regulations and administration.

Chapter III proposes a strategy to leverage FDI as a catalyst for national competitiveness and sustainable development. Four determinants of national competitiveness are identified: human capital, infrastructure, financial markets and the internationalization of local firms. Concrete measures to enhance the impact of FDI on these four determinants are proposed. These include proposals to attract FDI in higher education, in the development of ports and roads, and in capital markets. Measures to enhance linkages between local firms and foreign investors are also suggested. A strategy to promote "green and responsible" FDI is proposed, which could be tested at first in export-processing zones before being extended nationally. The strategy suggests building on international developments regarding environmental issues and corporate social responsibility, in order to define a unique profile for El Salvador. The consequences of the proposed strategies on investment promotion efforts are briefly touched upon.

Chapter IV highlights the main findings and recommendations of the review.

I. FDI TRENDS AND IMPACT

A. General background

El Salvador has gone a long way towards converting its once agriculture-based, mono-exporting economy into a modern, diversified and competitive economy. It is the smallest and most densely populated country in Central America, with an estimated population of 6.1 million. Its geography consists of a narrow fertile coastal plain, and volcanic upland in the interior. The Salvadorean economy is the fourth-largest in the region, with a nominal gross domestic product (GDP) of $22.1 billion in 2008. It is third in terms of per capita income, behind Costa Rica and Panama. Coming out of a civil war that ravaged the country for over a decade, the Peace Treaty of 1992 marked the beginning of a new era for socio-economic development in El Salvador.

Consecutive administrations since the end of the war have implemented reforms to modernize and open the economy to international trade and investment. The policies adopted included privatization, dollarization, and the conclusion of free-trade agreements. The smooth and peaceful transition of power in the 2009 presidential elections is testament to the maturity of El Salvador's democracy, and the new Government is committed to uphold the market-oriented policies. This holds promise for the socio-economic development of the country and should help foster a stronger and more positive image among the international business community.

1. Economic policies and performance

El Salvador's growth performance has been more or less in line with that of its neighbours in the recent past. After a period of rapid expansion in the immediate post-war period (1992–1995), annual real GDP growth stabilized at an average of 2.6 per cent in 1996–2004 (fig. I.1). Since 2005, economic performance has improved, with real GDP growth averaging almost 4 per cent per year, owing to increased consumer demand fuelled by remittances, strong commodity prices for traditional agricultural exports (coffee and sugar) and a rise in FDI. Partly as a consequence of the global economic and financial crisis, however, real GDP growth fell to 2.5 per cent in 2008 and is expected to slow down further in 2009.

Although the big shift in diversification and decreased dependence on agriculture occurred earlier in the twentieth century, the economy continued to diversify in the past decades. Manufacturing accounted for 24.2 per cent of GDP in 2008, up from 21.8 per cent in 1990 (fig. I.2). The sector is itself quite diversified, as no segment dominates. The maquila subsector (assembly for re-export) is the largest component of manufacturing, but still only represents 11 per cent of manufacturing output, or 2.7 per cent of GDP. Food processing (bakery, milling, sugar, beverages) also represents a significant share of the manufacturing sector, as do the chemical industry and textiles and apparels (outside of the maquila sector). The commercial sector, which includes retail, restaurants and hotels, is the second-largest component of the economy, representing 21.5 per cent of GDP in 2008.

Although the share of agriculture has been on a declining trend for decades, it remains an important component of the economy, with a 14 per cent share of GDP. Its importance in terms of employment and income for the poor is even bigger. Agriculture employs nearly a quarter of the labour force and it generates a third of export earnings, with coffee and sugar as the leading agro-exports. It is estimated that the sector meets about 70 per cent of domestic food needs.

Figure I.I. Real GDP growth, 1991–2008
(percentage)

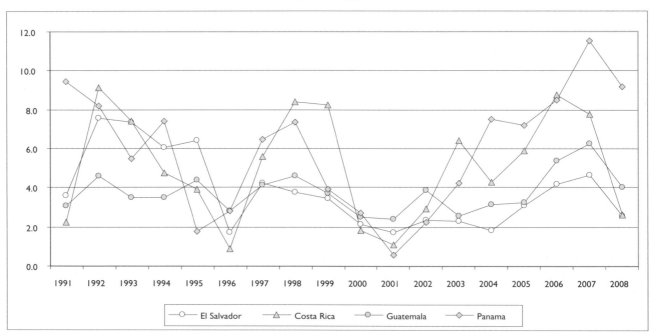

Sources: Banco Central de Reserva de El Salvador (BCR) and IMF.

Figure I.2. GDP composition by economic activity, 1990–2008
(percentage of the total)

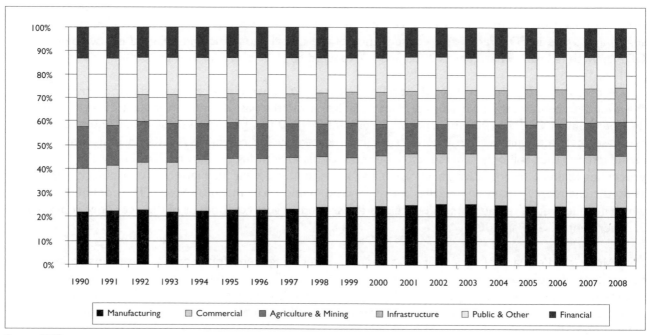

Source: BCR.

The infrastructure sector has performed well and currently represents 14 per cent of GDP, with transport, storage and communication being by far the largest components. Within the financial sector, which accounts for 12 per cent of GDP, the output of banks and insurance companies has steadily increased, and has been a key element in the diversification of the Salvadorean economy into services. Finally, government spending has been historically low in El Salvador, and it fell further from 7.4 per cent to 4.9 per cent of GDP between 1990 and 2008.

Economic growth has translated into some gains in terms of standards of living, as can be attested by the country's Human Development Index performance. El Salvador has consistently ranked third in Central America after Costa Rica and Panama, and ranks 106th out of 182 in the 2009 Human Development Report.[1] The same is true for the Human Poverty Index, where El Salvador ranks 64th out of 135, well below Panama (28th) and Costa Rica (10th).

Despite the steady increase in real GDP over the past couple of decades, over a quarter of the population still lives on less than two dollars a day. Purchasing power parity gross national income (GNI) per capita was $6,670 in 2008. This places El Salvador third in Central America, above Nicaragua ($2,620), Honduras ($3,870) and Guatemala ($4,690); but far from Costa Rica ($10,950) and Panama ($11,650). In addition, income inequality remains significant, with the share of income held by the poorest 20 per cent of the population stable in the past decade at around 3 per cent.

By contrast, El Salvador has improved in terms of access to healthcare and education. Life expectancy at birth has increased to 71.5 years, and the number of physicians per 1,000 people has risen too. In addition, enrolment in primary education now reaches 96 per cent.

One of the driving factors behind the relatively small gains in fighting poverty is the low level of savings in the country. The Salvadorean economy has long been characterized by low levels of capital formation, and, especially since the 1990s, by extremely high relative levels of consumption, fuelled mainly by remittances. While household consumption represented 85 per cent of gross national income (GNI), gross fixed capital formation (GFCF) averaged less than 14 per cent of GNI in the past five years, of which 12 per cent was private investment (fig. I.3). As a comparison, the high-growth "Asian tigers" have had sustained GFCF in excess of 30 per cent of GDP for quite a few decades.

Figure I.3. Composition of gross national disposable income
(in millions of dollars)

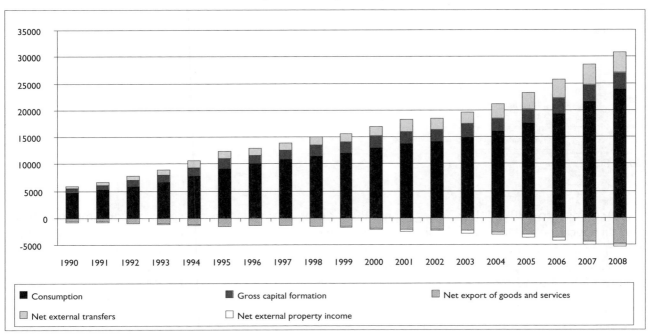

Source: BCR.

---

[1] The Human Development Index measures welfare in terms of education, health and standard of living. El Salvador is in the medium development range, above Honduras (112th), Guatemala (122nd) and Nicaragua (124th), but well below Panama (60th) and Costa Rica (54th).

The modest levels of capital formation in El Salvador are insufficient to sustain rates of GDP growth that would more significantly and rapidly improve the living standards of the population and markedly reduce poverty. The challenge to the government is how to boost and support domestic investment together with its strategy to attract more FDI. Although it has not been the case thus far, the large inflows of remittances that currently fuel high levels of consumption could potentially contribute to an increase in domestic investment.

The civil war and poor socio-economic conditions drove many Salvadoreans out of the country. Official figures estimate that there are close to 3 million Salvadoreans abroad, including 2.6 million in the United States alone.[2] These emigrants contribute heavily to the Salvadorean economy through remittances. The flow of remittances to El Salvador reached $3.8 billion in 2008 ($618 per capita), equivalent to 17 per cent of GDP (fig. I.4). Remittances have increased by almost 80 per cent in the past five years, and similarly to other countries in Latin America, the flow of remittances widely surpasses FDI inflows. While they contribute enormously to the revenue of the poorer segments of the population, remittances also present a macroeconomic challenge for recipient countries, which need to channel external savings to increase productive capacity and avoid inflationary pressures and "Dutch disease".[3]

Figure I.4. Remittances from Salvadoreans abroad
(in millions of dollars; and as a percentage of household disposable income)

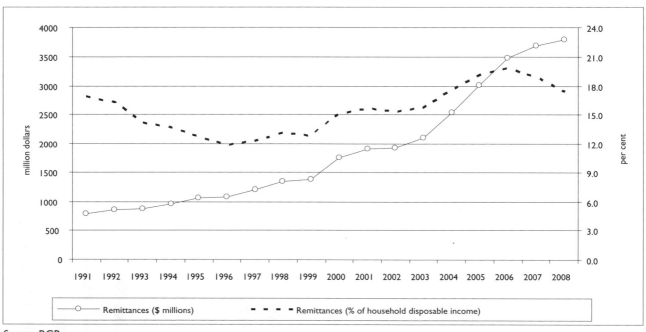

Source: BCR.

According to a 2006 IMF working paper,[4] 80 per cent of remittances are spent on consumption, 15 per cent on education and health, and only 5 per cent on investment and savings. This has led to a widening trade deficit, owing to consistently higher imports financed by remittances than export earnings. The current financial crisis has negatively affected the flow of remittances, which fell by 11 per cent in the first seven months of 2009 to $2.0 billion, compared with $2.3 billion in the same period in 2008.

---

[2] The Ministry of Foreign Relations reports that there are 2,964,004 Salvadoreans living abroad. The regional breakdown is as follows: North America: 2,756,316; Central America and the Caribbean: 142,652; Europe: 43,391; South America: 2,345; rest of the world: 19,300.

[3] In this case, increases in revenue due to remittances may deindustrialize the nation's economy by raising domestic prices of non-tradable goods, which makes traditional export industries in the manufacturing sector less competitive.

[4] Cáceres, Luis René and Saca, Nolvia N (2006).

Over the past decades, El Salvador has implemented sound macroeconomic policies, resulting in economic stability and sustaining moderate growth. As a first step, the country underwent an important privatization process that liberalized the banking, electricity and telecommunications sectors as well as the pension system.

Secondly, the Government dollarized the economy in 2001.[5] As a consequence, El Salvador relinquished control over monetary, exchange rate and interest rate policies, and it had to forgo some seignorage revenue. The economy, however, was dollarized in order to reduce inflationary pressures, to lower real interest rates, and to provide long-term stability for investors. These goals have largely been achieved, and the new Government indicated from the outset that it had no intention of reconsidering the dollarization of the economy.

Thirdly, El Salvador has embraced trade liberalization and concluded several free trade agreements with key trading partners, including its Central American neighbours, and with Chile, Mexico, the United States, and Taiwan Province of China. The recently elected Government has pledged to continue the market-based reforms and the negotiations for free trade agreements with Canada and Colombia.

2.   The state of infrastructure

The quality and availability of infrastructure services in El Salvador have improved significantly in the past two decades. Heavy investments were required after the civil war, which caused damage estimated at \$1.6 billion to telecommunication lines, the electricity system and roads.[6] In addition, the subsequent earthquakes in 2001 and hurricanes in 2006 and 2009 severely affected public infrastructure in some regions.

Investments to improve the country's roads and ports infrastructure have been executed, and were financed mostly by the public sector, with funds from multilateral financial institutions or development banks. However, the Government has been willing to contract out projects, and has begun to offer larger concessions that require private investment, including FDI. Meanwhile, the private sector has invested heavily in electricity and telecommunications.

El Salvador has a very good network of roads, which is ranked as number 36 in the world and second-best in Latin America, behind only Chile, according to the World Economic Forum 2008/2009 *Global Competitiveness Report*. There are over 6,600 kilometres of roads in the country, half of which are paved, and two main highways running almost parallel to each other from West to East. They are connected by a road that runs through San Salvador, and converge in La Unión in the Fonseca Gulf in the eastern end of the country, where a new port has been built with the support of the Government of Japan, but which is not operational yet.

The Pan-American Highway crosses the country from Guatemala to the eastern Honduran border, connecting El Salvador's major cities of Santa Ana, San Miguel and San Salvador (the capital). The Carretera del Litoral runs south along the Pacific coast, connecting the ports of Acajutla and La Unión. In addition, a third highway is under planning and construction. When completed, it will span from Guatemala to Honduras, along El Salvador's northern border. This project is funded by the Millennium Challenge Corporation, which granted \$461 million to El Salvador over a period of five years to fund development projects, with the largest share of \$234 million going to transport. In addition, the grant will serve to improve 240 kilometres of unpaved roads throughout the country. Likewise, a major ring road around San Salvador is under planning.

El Salvador has two ports: Acajutla in the south-west, and La Unión in the Fonseca Gulf in the east, but only the former is operational. Acajutla is located 85km west of San Salvador and specializes in bulk cargo. In

---

[5] The dollar was introduced as legal tender in 2001 at a fixed rate of 8.75 colones to the dollar.
[6] World Bank (2003).

2007, it handled 4.4 million tons of cargo and has experienced a continuous 20 per cent growth rate in the past five years. Infrastructure is minimal at Acajutla. It does not have port-side cranes, yet the services are relatively efficient. Ships docked at Acajutla were idle only 8 per cent of the time in 2008, and it processed 336 tons per effective work-hour on average. The port is well below modern standards of infrastructure, however, and it does not have the capacity to become a regional hub.

In order to remedy the physical and technical limitations of Acajutla and develop a port with the capacity to become a regional hub, El Salvador first considered, in 1994, building a new port in La Unión. Following pre-feasibility studies, the Japan Bank for International Cooperation granted a ¥11.2 billion official development assistance (ODA) loan for the construction of the port, which began in 2005 and was completed at the end of 2008. Although the core infrastructure (wharf, container terminal, multi-purpose terminal, roll-on roll-off terminal, administrative building) has been completed and officially handed over to the Government by the construction consortium, the port is not yet operational, for lack of an operator. While it is generally agreed that the port should be concessioned, there remain many stumbling blocks on how the concession should be structured – possibly through a private–public partnership agreement.

According to the WEF's 2008/2009 *Global Competitiveness Report*, El Salvador has the third-best airport infrastructure in Latin America, surpassed only by Chile and Panama. There are four airports with paved runways in the country, the most important of which is El Salvador International Airport (Comalapa Airport). The airport handled more than 2 million passengers and 29,000 tons of cargo in 2007. It is also the main hub for the Salvadorean airline TACA, which has a network connecting over 40 cities in 20 countries in the Americas, and which transported more than 6 million passengers that same year.

A renovation project for El Salvador's main airport is planned. This would include construction of a new passenger terminal and expansion of the maintenance area. The Japan Bank for International Cooperation may finance the construction of the new terminal. The second-largest airport, Ilopango Airport, is located on the eastern edge of San Salvador, and it is currently reserved for military aviation and private use.

The infrastructure of the information and communications technology (ICT) sector in El Salvador has improved markedly in recent years. The number of fixed telephone lines has almost tripled in the past decade, bringing the total number to 1.1 million in 2008, which translates into 17.5 lines per 100 people.[7] More impressive is the growth in mobile telephony that has been entirely upgraded to GSM technology. Today, the number of mobile subscriptions is more than six times higher than the number of fixed lines. With 113 mobile phones per 100 people, El Salvador has the highest teledensity[8] in Central America. Internet services in El Salvador have effectively migrated to broadband technology, while older technologies have all but disappeared. About 99 per cent of the 142,000 internet subscriptions in the country are broadband, with close to 67 per cent using xDSL technology.

El Salvador's electricity infrastructure was severely damaged during the civil war. The authorities subsequently invested heavily to restore the country's transmission and distribution network. Today, El Salvador has a total installed capacity of 1,422 megawatts (MW) with net generation of 5,716 gigawatt-hours (GWh), and it enjoys a national electrification coverage rate of 83 per cent, which is among the best in the region. It is estimated that the average electrification in urban centres is 97 per cent, whereas coverage in rural areas is 72 per cent.

El Salvador shares transmission interconnections with its two neighbours, and historically, it has been a net importer of electricity. Supplied mostly from Guatemala, electricity imports peaked in 2000, when they represented 17 per cent of total demand. Finally, El Salvador is part of the SIEPAC[9] regional interconnection

---

[7] Based on a population of 6.13 million people.

[8] Mobile plus fixed lines per capita.

[9] SIEPAC stands for Sistema de Interconexión para América Central. The participating countries are: Costa Rica, El Salvador, Guatemala, Honduras, Nicaragua and Panama. The interconnection system will be operated by the Empresa Propietaria de la Red, a mixed-capital company of which 75 per cent is owned by public entities from the six countries and 25 per cent is owned by Endesa of Spain and ISA of Colombia.

project, which is near completion. Once in operation, SIEPAC will allow the international sale of electricity throughout Central America, effectively creating a single regional electricity market.

3.   The state of education and skills

Despite some recent improvements, education indicators remain unsatisfactory in El Salvador. Coverage and quality are inadequate, and historically, public spending on education has been among the lowest in Central America, averaging 2.8 per cent of GDP in the 2000–2005 period. The Government has recognized the shortcomings in public education and has pledged to invest more to improve the quality of education. The result has been the creation of the *Plan Nacional de Educación 2021*, a long-term roadmap for the development of the educational system with an emphasis on fostering scientific and technical studies. Plan 2021 aims to achieve the standards set by the Millennium Development Goals by: (a) providing equitable access to education; (b) improving the effectiveness of education; (c) promoting educational competitiveness; and (d) setting best practices in management.

The Ministry of Education estimates that 93 per cent of children between the ages of 7 and 12 attend school. Enrolment rates in 2009 in primary, secondary and tertiary education were 96 per cent, 42 per cent and 25 per cent respectively. The population aged between 15 and 24, whose education was not affected by the civil war, has, on average, 8.3 years of formal education, and their literacy rate is 96 per cent, whereas the 25 to 59 age group received, on average, only 7.4 years of formal education, and has a literacy rate of 87 per cent.

Investment in education rose from 3.1 per cent of GDP in 2003 to 4.2 per cent in 2009, and as a percentage of total government expenditure it grew from 16.8 per cent to 23.1 per cent. In comparison, Costa Rica, Guatemala and the Dominican Republic spent 4.9 per cent, 3.1 per cent and 2.4 per cent of their GDP respectively in 2007. The increase in funds for the public education system in El Salvador is reflected in some indicators. Today, 85 per cent of students have access to running water and electricity in their school, as opposed to 78 per cent in 2004. Also, 60 per cent of students in secondary education have access to the internet in their school, compared to 44 per cent in 2004. There are 6,263 educational centres – of which 1,100 are private institutions – providing education from pre-school to high school in the country. In addition, there are 24 universities, and 8 technological and 6 specialized institutions of higher learning.

4.   Security issues

Threats to personal security and the high general level of violence have a very detrimental effect not only on workers, but also on the cost of doing business. Workers, in particular at a lower level of income, suffer the impact of violence the most directly. Extortions and assaults on public transport are widespread throughout the country.

In addition to the social impact on workers, investors report that the high level of violence significantly affects the cost of doing business in El Salvador. Although it is rarely a reason to prevent foreign companies from investing in the country, violence clearly affects competitiveness. In a recent survey of more than 100 companies conducted on behalf of PROESA,[10] it emerged that security was considered the most significant obstacle to operating a business, well ahead of access to finance.

Close to 70 per cent of companies surveyed indicated that the cost of protecting themselves against violence amounted to between 1 and 5 per cent of turnover. For almost 20 per cent of companies, the

---

[10] Encuesta clima de negocios El Salvador, septiembre–noviembre 2009, Herratemarketing. The survey included 128 companies, of which 53 per cent were foreign investors.

Table I.I. Comparative FDI flows with selected countries, 1991–2008
(dollars and percentages)

Country	ABSOLUTE PERFORMANCE					RELATIVE PERFORMANCE													
	FDI inflows (Millions of dollars)				FDI stock	FDI inflows												FDI stock
						Per capita (dollars)				Per $1000 GDP				As per cent of gross fixed capital formation				Per capita ($)	Percentage of GDP
	Average (1991–1995)	Average (1996–2000)	Average (2001–2005)	Average (2006–2008)	2008	Average (1991–1995)	Average (1996–2000)	Average (2001–2005)	Average (2006–2008)	Average (1991–1995)	Average (1996–2000)	Average (2001–2005)	Average (2006–2008)	Average (1991–1995)	Average (1996–2000)	Average (2001–2005)	Average (2006–2008)	2008	2008
El Salvador	19.4	309.4	353.0	844.6	6701.4	3.6	50.9	53.0	118.3	2.8	25.5	23.1	40.8	1.6	15.3	14.4	25.9	926.7	30.3
Chile	1666.1	5666.9	5042.7	12220.8	100988.5	118.4	376.7	314.9	732.8	29.9	74.0	58.3	75.2	12.3	31.9	28.6	35.2	6010.2	59.6
Colombia	911.9	3089.4	3932.7	8756.2	67228.9	24.4	76.4	87.8	186.1	13.5	31.3	33.3	42.7	6.4	17.0	17.1	17.6	1411.8	27.7
Costa Rica	257.1	494.7	669.9	1795.4	10818.0	77.2	131.9	159.8	401.4	26.8	35.2	37.2	69.0	13.9	19.2	19.8	31.2	2385.8	36.3
Dominican Republic	227.0	701.5	928.1	1997.3	11408.0	30.3	86.5	107.4	217.7	17.4	32.9	37.4	48.2	11.0	16.7	22.4	26.3	1230.2	25.1
Guatemala	93.5	243.7	354.3	724.8	5455.4	9.8	22.7	29.5	54.6	9.3	14.5	15.9	21.1	5.4	7.5	8.6	10.4	402.5	14.0
Honduras	52.5	187.1	425.7	787.3	5112.2	9.9	30.1	61.3	104.5	14.5	29.3	49.4	63.4	6.2	11.1	20.3	21.5	665.7	36.2
Jamaica	155.6	349.7	619.5	845.9	9456.2	64.0	136.8	235.8	316.6	37.4	46.0	71.7	72.3	13.0	17.6	23.6	23.1	3524.8	65.7
Mauritius	17.1	86.0	24.3	275.7	1631.7	15.6	73.2	19.7	217.0	5.1	19.3	4.1	35.5	1.8	8.1	1.9	13.8	1277.0	19.3
Mexico	6808.4	13285.6	23115.9	22847.9	294680.1	75.7	136.3	222.1	208.4	19.5	29.9	33.9	21.7	10.8	14.8	17.2	9.8	2658.7	27.1
Nicaragua	47.9	206.1	209.3	431.5	3755.6	11.2	42.9	39.6	75.1	15.7	56.5	48.4	73.3	8.2	20.7	18.4	24.9	643.9	59.1
Panama	209.4	896.5	643.9	2268.9	16973.9	81.0	316.0	204.2	679.0	25.2	83.8	46.6	115.4	14.7	39.6	28.4	56.7	4993.9	72.6
Sri Lanka	123.1	218.0	220.4	611.9	4282.6	6.7	11.2	10.8	29.0	11.6	14.2	11.4	18.0	4.6	5.6	5.3	7.2	201.6	10.5
CAFTA-DR (non-US)	697.5	2142.5	2940.4	6581.0	43250.6	19.7	54.0	67.2	139.0	14.9	28.9	31.3	46.7	8.3	14.5	16.8	22.	899.1	27.6
Developing countries	77905.9	202786.2	239031.0	527947.1	4275982.0	18.0	43.1	47.2	98.8	15.7	31.1	28.7	35.6	6.4	13.1	11.6	13.0	791.2	24.8

Source: UNCTAD FDI/TNC database.

cost is estimated at between 6 and 10 per cent. Although El Salvador is not unique in Central America in this respect, the social and economic costs of violence are very high, and the issue needs to be forcefully addressed by the Government. It is not within the brief of this report or the competence of UNCTAD to offer recommendations on how to fight organized crime and violence. Improvements in the investment environment nevertheless call for significant efforts on that front.

B. FDI trends, performance and impact

1. Overall FDI trends and performance

El Salvador attracted $5.9 billion of cumulative FDI inflows in the period 1992–2008, an average of $350 million per year. It ranks third in Central America, far behind Panama ($15.5 billion) and Costa Rica ($12.3 billion), and only marginally higher than Guatemala and Honduras. Annual FDI inflows per capita averaged $57.8 in El Salvador in this 17-year period, more than Honduras ($49.5) or Nicaragua ($39.9), but considerably less than Costa Rica ($176) and Panama ($293.9). Aside from two peak years, FDI inflows have been relatively modest in absolute terms, but comparable to the developing countries average in relative terms, i.e. on a per capita basis or in relation to GDP (table 1.1). As highlighted by the situation of Costa Rica, Panama and other countries, however, many small economies have succeeded in attracting significantly higher inflows of FDI in relative terms, which indicates that El Salvador could fare much better in the future if the conditions were right.

Figure 1.5. FDI inflows to El Salvador, Costa Rica, Honduras and Panama, 1995–2008

(in millions of dollars)

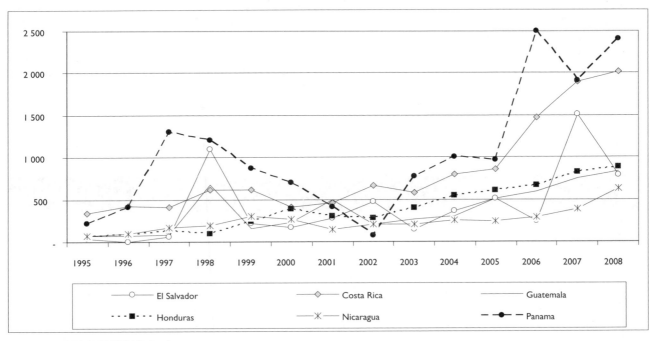

Source: UNCTAD, FDI/TNC database.

Prior to the 1990s there was very little foreign investment in El Salvador, in part due to the civil war. Annual flows never surpassed $30 million, and the country experienced negative net inflows in the late 1970s and early 1980s due in large part to the civil war. Between 1970 and 1991, the country attracted cumulative FDI flows of merely $254 million. As El Salvador emerged from the civil war and sought to attract foreign investors, it began to receive larger amounts of FDI, which have had an increasing influence on the economy.

Progressively, FDI as a percentage of GFCF has grown from an average of 1.6 per cent in 1991–1995 to 25.9 per cent in 2006–2008.[11]

The country's market-oriented policies took effect after the privatization of several state entities and El Salvador experienced some gains in FDI, however the growth in inflows has not been steady. In 1998, privatizations in electricity and telecommunications led to a one-time large inflow of FDI, as foreign investors spent close to $600 million to gain control over the country's electricity distribution companies and $316 million to acquire the state-owned telecom provider. The second year of windfall inflows was 2007, which saw FDI inflows in excess of $1.5 billion, predominantly in the financial sector. Citibank and HSBC entered the Salvadorean market through several acquisitions (fig. 1.5).

2. Distribution by sector and countries of origin

Although there are registered foreign investors of over 24 different nationalities, the source countries of FDI in El Salvador are highly concentrated. More than half of all FDI in the period 1998–2008 has come from two countries. The United States accounts for roughly 30 per cent of all FDI inflows, and Panama represents another 26 per cent. Other important investments come from the British Virgin Islands (7 per cent), Spain (3 per cent) and Canada (3 per cent).

There are several important transnational corporations (TNCs) with well-known brands, including in the telecommunication, retail, and consumer goods sectors. The telecommunications market in El Salvador is highly competitive and is an important destination for FDI. Companies such as América Móvil, Digicel, Millicom (Tigo) and Telefónica have multi-million dollar investments in the region. American retail giants Wal-Mart and PriceSmart are also leading players in El Salvador and neighbouring countries, with over $3.3 billion in total income in 2007 for the region as a whole (table 1.2). In addition, the consumer goods market has attracted considerable investment from global conglomerates such as Kimberley-Clark and Unilever. Extraregional TNCs in other sectors are Swiss food giant Nestlé, Mexican cement manufacturer Cemex, and German pharmaceutical company Bayer, with $735 million, $662 million and $330 million respectively in income for their Central American operations in 2007. FDI from TNCs in neighbouring countries is concentrated in food and beverages, along with significant investments in electronics and pharmaceuticals.

Table 1.2. Top 20 non-financial foreign companies with a presence in El Salvador, 2007

(in millions of dollars)

Company name	Country of origin	Sector	Regional income*
América Móvil	Mexico	Telecom	3 392
Wal-Mart	United States	Retail	2 534
Digicel	Jamaica	Telecom	1 500
Millicom	Luxembourg	Telecom	1 149
AES	United States	Electricity	1 130
Telefónica	Spain	Telecom	918
PriceSmart	United States	Retail	869
Nestlé	Switzerland	Food	735
Kimberley-Clark	United States	Consumer goods	677
Cemex	Mexico	Cement	662
Grupo Monge	Costa Rica	Electric appliances	505

[11] The ratio of FDI flows to GFCF must be analysed with care. FDI data include flows generated by the purchase of local assets by foreigners, including through cross-border mergers and acquisitions. Such flows do not lead to the creation of new capital stock. As a result, a given ratio of FDI to GFCF does not mean that foreign investors are actually responsible for that percentage of GFCF. If mergers and acquisitions (e.g. under a privatization programme) are significant, the ratio overestimates the role of foreign investors in GFCF.

Company name	Country of origin	Sector	Regional income*
Femsa	Mexico	Beverages	475
CabCorp	Guatemala	Beverages	452
Unilever	United Kingdom	Consumer goods	410
Pollo Campero	Guatemala	Restaurant	380
Fifco	Costa Rica	Beverages	374
Bayer	Germany	Pharmaceuticals	330
Blue Oil	United Kingdom	Fossil fuels	234
Grupo Melo	Panama	Food	220
Cefa	Costa Rica	Pharmaceuticals	200
TOTAL			17 654

* *Operations in Central America and the Caribbean, not limited to El Salvador.*
Source: Estrategia y Negocios.

FDI flows have been concentrated in four key sectors over the past couple of decades: (a) finance; (b) telecommunications; (c) manufacturing; and (d) electricity. This is attested by the shares they represent in the stock of FDI as of 2008 (fig. I.6). Although finance has the largest share, with 28 per cent of the total, FDI in the sector is a relatively recent phenomenon that peaked with very large investments in banking in 2007. FDI in telecommunications is on a par with FDI in manufacturing, each representing 14 per cent of the total stock. Foreign investors became involved in telecommunications with the privatization of the state-owned monopoly in the late 1990s, and subsequently continued to invest significantly to develop the mobile phone and internet network (section B.6). Investments in manufacturing were significant too, and relatively diversified.

Figure I.6. Sectoral composition of FDI stocks, 2008
(percentage of the total)

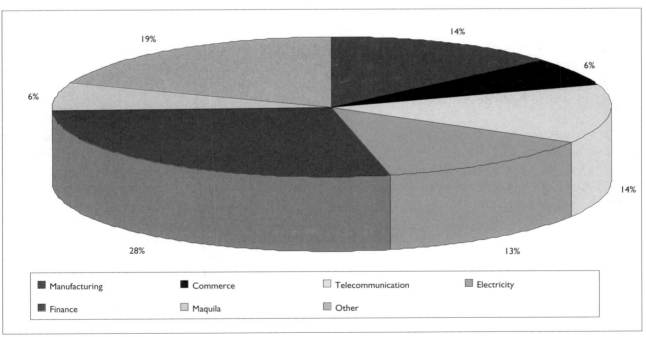

Source: BCR.

FDI in electricity was very significant in the late 1990s, when the state-owned monopoly was disaggregated and the power generation and distribution functions privatized. Although it draws significant attention, FDI in export processing zones (maquilas) only represents 6.3 per cent of total FDI stock – less than half the share of industry, and comparable to that of commerce. Foreign investments in other sectors are quite diverse, including in other services, construction and agriculture.

The following sections provide a more detailed analysis of the trends and economic impact of FDI on a sectoral basis. The maquila sector is considered separately, regardless of the activities that take place in the export processing zones.

3. FDI in manufacturing and agriculture

Cumulative FDI flows in manufacturing over the past two decades represent $920 million. El Salvador has specialized in light manufacturing, and until a few years ago, the textile industry dominated the manufacturing sector. More recently, the country has been able to attract significant foreign investments in electronics, auto parts and agro-industry, which have contributed to the diversification of the manufacturing sector.

El Salvador has successfully developed and is especially competitive in four niche markets in electronics: (a) electronic components; (b) home appliances and computer peripherals; (c) cable and harnesses assembly; and (d) medical apparatus. AVX – part of the Japanese Kyocera consortium – has long been present in El Salvador and has grown to be a leading company in the country, operating seven different assembly lines, exporting $120 million worth of products per year, and employing nearly 3,000 people. The Salvadorean branch of AVX absorbed the production chains of several other affiliates when plants in Mexico and the Czech Republic closed. As a result, more sophisticated assembly processes with higher value added are taking place in the country. At the beginning, AVX El Salvador was dedicated solely to assembling imported chips, whereas today the production chain has vertically integrated and even the chemical processes necessary to manufacture capacitors take place locally. This represents an important contribution to the development of human capital and employment for high-skilled workers.

In agro-industry, the Spanish group Calvo has invested over $100 million since 2003, when it opened a processing plant for canned tuna in La Unión. It employs 750 people and has an annual production capacity of 65,000 tons, mostly destined for the international market. Calvo was the second-largest exporter in 2007, corresponding to a total value of $98 million, up 58 per cent from the previous year. Other examples of FDI in agro-industry worth mentioning are Mexican fruit juice manufacturer Jumex, and the German supplier of ornamental plants, Red Fox.

Jumex entered the Salvadorean market in 2006, with an initial investment of $20 million that went into building a state-of-the-art processing and bottling plant whose construction was finalized in 2008. The company has 118 employees in El Salvador and exports to over 20 countries, including to Mexico and to Central American and Caribbean countries. Jumex El Salvador also serves as the company's distribution centre in Central America.

Part of the Dümmen Group, Red Fox is a specialized breeder and producer of young ornamental plants that opened operations in El Salvador in 2007 with an initial investment of $25 million. The company has built 5 out of 20 planned greenhouses and has taken advantage of its free zone status to export plants to the United States and Canada. Currently, the company has 500 employees as part of the construction phase, and it plans to expand its number of employees to anywhere between 1,000 and 1,500 people.

As the above cases illustrate, FDI in manufacturing has been diversified, and has mostly been in niche markets. While some global TNCs have invested in the sector, most foreign investors are smaller and have a more limited reach. Attracting niche investors and smaller TNCs makes FDI promotion efforts more difficult, but this is a situation that all small countries must confront. By their essence, niches are more complex to identify for the authorities; this makes it all the more essential to provide a good overall investment climate and competitive operational conditions.

4.   FDI in banking and finance

Banking and finance have attracted $1.9 billion of inflows in the past two decades. The vast majority of this was in 2007 and 2008. Even so, foreign investors became involved in the financial sector as soon as the banking system was re-privatized in 1990. Several mergers and acquisitions then consolidated the position of foreign investors in finance in the country, and today they own a majority stake in every private bank in El Salvador.

Out of the 10 major commercial banks operating in the country, two remain state-owned: the Banco de Fomento Agropecuario, which was created in 1973 to promote investment in agriculture, and the Banco Hipotecario, which was created in 1934 to finance mortgages and foster small and medium-size enterprises. The other eight commercial banks are private, and foreign investors have a majority stake in each of them (table 1.3).

Banco Agrícola is El Salvador's largest bank, with nearly 30 per cent of the market share. Through several acquisitions, Banco Agrícola has consolidated its position as the market leader. Bancolombia acquired 99 per cent of the capital of Banco Agrícola in 2006 and 2007 for $890 million.

Citibank expanded its operations in El Salvador by registering a new commercial bank separate from its Citibank N.A. branch already present in the country. The new entity, Banco Citibank de El Salvador, became the second-largest bank when it absorbed Banco Cuscatlán and Banco Uno in 2007. Grupo Cuscatlán, previously the second-largest bank in El Salvador, was acquired for a reported $1.5 billion, while Grupo Financiero Uno, the largest credit-card issuer in Central America which included Banco Uno El Salvador, was purchased for $2.1 billion.

HSBC entered the Central American financial sector after buying Banistmo, the largest bank in Panama, for $1.7 billion in 2006, which itself owned a 56 per cent stake in Banco Salvadoreño. A year later, HSBC offered $190.7 million to secure a 97 per cent ownership of the bank. After this transaction, Banco Salvadoreño changed its name to Banco HSBC Salvadoreño and became the third-largest bank in the country.

Table 1.3. Commercial banks in El Salvador, 2008

Bank	Nationality of investor	Assets (in billions of dollars)	Market share (percentage)
Banco Agrícola	Colombia	3.90	29.0
Banco Citibank de El Salvador	United States	2.73	20.3
Banco HSBC Salvadoreño	United Kingdom	2.11	15.7
Scotiabank	Canada	2.10	15.7
Banco de América Central	United States	1.05	7.8
Banco Hipotecario*	El Salvador	0.39	2.9
Banco Promerica	Nicaragua	0.39	2.9
Banco Procredit	Germany	0.26	2.0
Banco de Fomento Agropecuario*	El Salvador	0.21	1.6
Banco G&T Continental	Guatemala	0.15	1.1
TOTAL		13.45	100.0

State-owned banks.
Source: Economist Intelligence Unit.

The Bank of Nova Scotia was the first international bank to gain a majority ownership in a Salvadorean bank. The Canadian bank acquired an initial 53 per cent interest in Banco Ahorromet for an estimated $24 million in 1997. Three years later, it increased its stake to 98.3 per cent of capital, and Ahorromet became Scotiabank El Salvador. In May 2005, Scotiabank El Salvador consolidated its position as the fourth-largest bank in the country by acquiring Banco de Comercio for $178 million.

Banco de América Central is a regional bank that operates in all six Central American countries, with the holding company headquartered in Panama. Banco de América Central entered El Salvador in 1997 after merging with Credomatic Group, an entity specialized in credit card financing, with operations in Honduras and El Salvador. GE Capital Global Banking first purchased 49.9 per cent of Banco de América Central in 2005 and increased its stake in the bank to 75 per cent in June 2009. The amounts paid for the transactions were not disclosed.

It is still early to assess the full impact of the dominance of foreign investors in banking, as they have been present in El Salvador for only a couple of years and mostly at a time of global financial crisis. And yet, a number of local entrepreneurs have pointed out that since foreign investors took control of the banking system, it has become more difficult to obtain financing for investment. With headquarters outside of El Salvador and decisions on large investment loans taken outside the country, local investors feel that it has become more difficult to present projects, and that decision-makers are unaware of local business conditions.

In addition, some foreign banks are more heavily focused on lucrative retail banking and consumer credits than on industrial lending. Disaggregated data on outstanding bank loans partially support this claim, as loans to businesses have decreased as a percentage of total loans while consumer lending (housing and consumption) have notably increased (fig. I.7). However, it must be stressed that this trend was well set before major foreign investments occurred in 2006 and 2007 when HSBC and Citibank entered the market. In turn, there are no signs that foreign-owned banks are reversing this trend in lending.

Figure I.7. Sectoral composition of bank loans, 2003–2008

(percentage of outstanding loans)

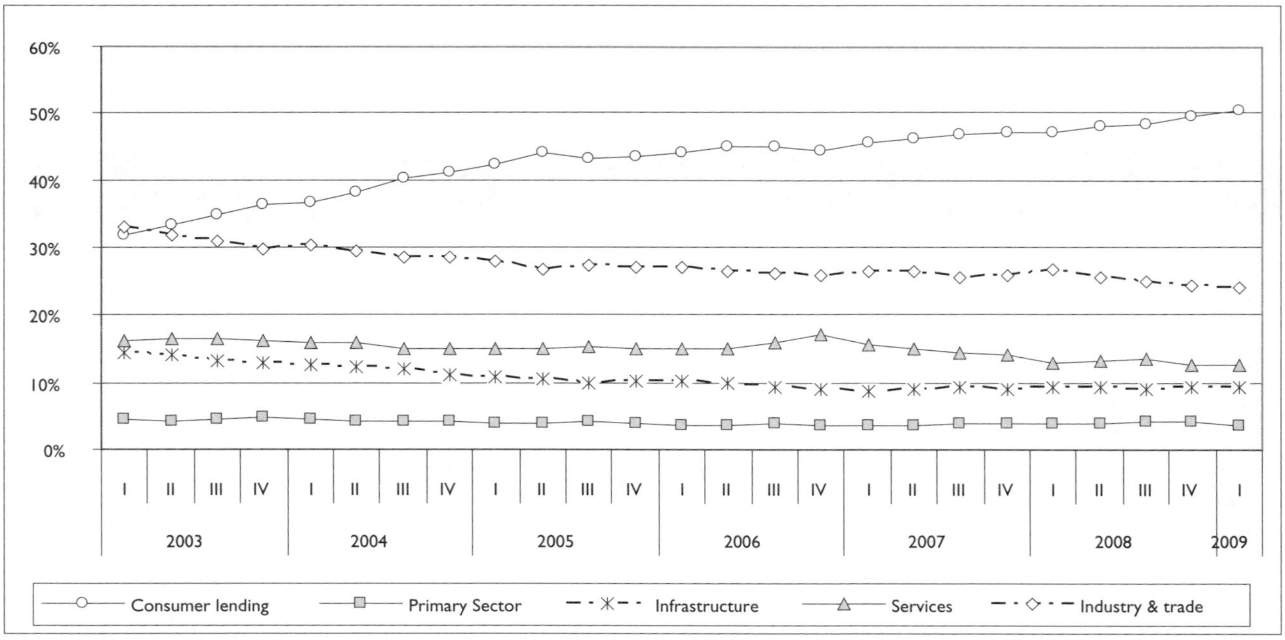

Source: Superintendencia del Sistema Financiero.

Outstanding consumer loans (housing and consumption) increased by 144 per cent between the first quarter of 2003 and the first quarter of 2009, at a time when total outstanding loans only rose by 54 per cent. As a result, the relative share of consumer loans increased to 50.5 per cent of total bank loans in the first quarter of 2009, from 31.9 per cent six years earlier. More ready access to mortgage financing is a positive development for the population at large. At the same time, however, consumption credits skyrocketed, which may entail a higher level of personal and systemic risk, particularly in a country where a significant share of consumption is fed by remittances.[12]

In contrast, outstanding loans to the productive sectors increased a mere 12 per cent between the first quarter of 2003 and the first quarter of 2009, i.e. at a significantly lower rate than nominal GDP, which increased almost 50 per cent in the same period. As a consequence, the share of bank loans to the productive sector fell from 68.1 per cent to 49.5 per cent. Similarly to many countries in the region and other countries at a similar level of development, El Salvador suffers from a relatively poor system of financial intermediation, and access to credit for investment is not satisfactory. Although it is still a relatively recent phenomenon, the presence of foreign banks does not seem to have solved the problem. However, it cannot be concluded either that they have made the situation worse.

Foreign ownership of domestic banks partly increases El Salvador's exposure to global financial crises. The current financial crisis severely affected the global financial institutions present in El Salvador, which may have led them to tighten their lending practices in the country as part of an overall review of their positions and that of their affiliates.

One area where the presence of foreign banks appears to have been positive is in terms of the cost of remittances. Banks with a global presence have the possibility of passing on lower transaction costs for international transfers to their customers. In part, this seems to have been the case, particularly with respect to flows from the United States. The World Bank reports that the average cost of remittances between the United States and El Salvador is among the lowest in a series of bilateral "corridors" that are monitored on a systematic basis.[13] Although a bank such as Citibank does not offer special conditions on transfers from the United States to its affiliate in El Salvador, it does so with other developing countries. Aside from a foreign exchange margin, Citibank allows its customers to transfer money at no cost to a bank account in its affiliate in India or Mexico. Lower transaction costs are a large benefit to El Salvador, given that remittances exceed $3.5 billion per year.

The insurance sector is composed of 17 companies and one foreign insurance branch – the Pan-American Life Insurance Company. Five of these companies are specialized in life insurance, and the rest focus on property and casualty coverage. Most insurers are part of larger financial conglomerates aligned with the country's major banks. The insurance market is not as concentrated as banking, in part due to the fact that companies are specialized and that the market is still relatively small, with total assets estimated at $478 million, and there has not been clear consolidation. The top 10 insurers account for almost 90 per cent of the market.

Most insurance companies in El Salvador were acquired by foreign investors as part of the purchase of the major banks. SISA and SISA Vida, the largest property and life insurers respectively, were owned by Banco Cuscatlán. Likewise, the Scotiabank conglomerate owns Scotia Seguros and 99 per cent of Aseguradora Agrícola Comercial, HSBC owns HSBC Seguros Salvadoreños, and Bancolombia owns 50 per cent of Aseguradora Suiza Salvadoreña and 99 per cent of Asesuisa Vida through Banco Agrícola. The main exceptions to the rule are Pan-American and Aseguradora La Centroamericana, which is owned by Spanish insurer MAPFRE.

---

[12] Outstanding mortgage financing doubled between the first quarter of 2003 and the first quarter of 2009. Consumption credits, in turn, more than tripled during the same period.

[13] The average cost of transferring $500 from the United States to El Salvador is reported as the third-lowest among monitored corridors, at $10.2. See http://remittanceprices.worldbank.org.

5.   FDI in electricity

FDI in electricity amounted to $880 million in the past two decades, a significant amount given the size of the sector in El Salvador. Until the mid-1990s, the state-owned Comisión Hidroeléctrica del Río Lempa (CEL) was in charge of generation, transmission and distribution, under a vertically integrated public monopoly model. As part of the structural reform in the sector, the first step was to disaggregate distribution. Four regional distribution companies were constituted as private companies, with CEL as the majority stockholder: CLESA in the west, EEO in the east, DELSUR in the south and CAESS serving the greater San Salvador and north-central region.

In April 1997, the capital of the distribution companies was opened to the workers from the sector, who had a right as priority investors to 20 per cent of shares. A year later, 75 per cent of the capital of each company was auctioned at a public bidding. Foreign investors won the bidding for all four companies: ENERSAL (Bolivarian Republic of Venezuela) acquired CAESS and EEO for $297 million, Electricidad de Centroamérica (Chile) acquired DELSUR for $180 million, and AES (United States) acquired CLESA for $109 million. The remaining 5 per cent of stocks of each company were sold openly on the Salvadorean stock exchange.

The distribution sector has consolidated since then, and AES currently owns four of the five distribution companies (table 1.4). DELSUR is owned by another American company – Pennsylvania Power and Light. In addition, EDESAL, a small, locally owned company began distributing electricity mostly to rural and newly urbanized areas in 2006.

Table I.4. Distribution companies, 2008

Company	Owner	Total sales		Number of clients	
		GWh	percentage of total	thousands	percentage of total
CAESS	AES	1 988.3	43.8	512.8	36.3
DELSUR	PPL	1 158.9	25.5	305.8	21.6
CLESA	AES	797.5	17.6	300.1	21.2
EEO	AES	476.2	10.5	225.1	15.9
DEUSEM	AES	106.1	2.3	60.8	4.3
EDESAL	Salvadorean	14.2	0.3	8.1	0.6
TOTAL		4 541.2	100.0	1 412.7	100.0

Source: SIGET.

Generation was opened to private investment and FDI in 1999, but not all assets were privatized. CEL retains ownership of the country's major hydroelectric plants as a special autonomous public enterprise but ceded its thermal and geothermal operations. In 1999, the United States–based Duke Energy International bought CEL's entire thermal production facilities for $125 million. Meanwhile, that same year, LaGeo was created as a separate company to manage El Salvador's two geothermal plants. CEL remains the majority shareholder in LaGeo, although ENEL, the Italian energy company, has been an important partner in this mixed-capital enterprise. In 2002, ENEL acquired 12.5 per cent of LaGeo for a reported €26 million, and it currently owns 36 per cent of the shares, with the reserved right to eventually gain control over the company.[14] Another important generator in the wholesale market is Nejapa, a thermal plant owned by AES that accounts for 11 per cent of El Salvador's installed capacity (table I.5).

---

[14] ENEL sought to take a majority ownership of LaGeo in 2008, which was rejected by CEL. The case is currently under international arbitration with the International Chamber of Commerce.

Table I.5. Generation companies, 2008

Company	Type	Source	Installed capacity		Net generation	
			MW	percentage of total	GWh	percentage of total
CEL	Public	Hydroelectric	472.0	32.7	2 033.4	35.2
Duke	Private foreign	Thermal	338.3	23.5	810.2	14.0
LaGeo	Public/private	Geothermal	204.4	14.2	1 420.9	24.6
Nejapa	Private foreign	Thermal	144.0	10.0	521.1	9.0
CASSA	Private local	Thermal	60.0	4.2	98.2	1.7
Invers. Energ.	Private local	Thermal	51.2	3.6	312.9	5.4
Textufil	Private local	Thermal	44.1	3.1	182.0	3.1
CESSA	Private foreign	Thermal	32.6	2.3	191.9	3.3
Other			94.7	6.6	213.7	3.7
TOTAL			1 441.1	100.0	5 784.5	100.0

Source: SIGET.

Total installed capacity increased from 988 MW in 1999 when FDI in generation started, to 1,422 MW in 2008 – a 44 per cent jump. The private sector was responsible for most (350 MW) of the increased capacity, 27 per cent of which was FDI. Total private generation in the country has outstripped public generation since 2002, three years after the opening of the sector to private investment and FDI. Besides expanding generation capacity to meet demand, the restructuring of the sector and the introduction of private investment has also led to increased electrification coverage. Coverage has grown by 10 percentage points since distribution was taken over by foreign investors, and is above 83 per cent. Only Costa Rica and Panama have better coverage in the region (fig. I.8).

Figure I.8. Electrification coverage, 1985–2006

(percentage)

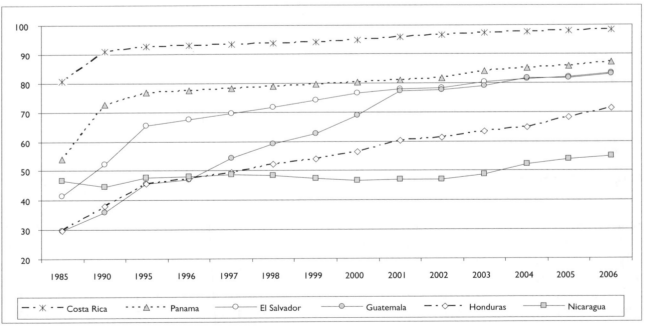

Source: Economic Commission for Latin American and the Caribbean.

Between 2002 and 2008, distribution companies took on an additional 250,000 clients. In parallel, the amount of electricity not served has declined, and the number of clients without meters has been cut dramatically. In contrast, the number of interruptions to individual clients and the number of customer complaints have steadily increased, even though this may be partly due to significantly more comprehensive recording, following the implementation of stricter regulatory standards in parallel with the privatization of the sector.

Salvadorean end-users continue to pay some of the highest prices for electricity in the region, with residential rates averaging $0.15 per kilowatt-hour. Production costs affected by exogenous factors, such as the rising price of fossil fuels, and by endogenous factors such as losses in the electricity system, all help to explain the relatively high prices. However, it is difficult to compare electricity prices across borders, because subsidies remain an important price distorter in the region. El Salvador – like the other countries in the region that have privatized their electricity sectors – has trimmed down its subsidies and consequently experienced a rise in prices. As a result, there has been a convergence in average residential prices for the four countries in the region that privatized (fig. I.9).[15] Starting March 2009, El Salvador stopped subsidizing residential consumption above 99 kWh per month,[16] and in a 2007 Letter of Intent to the International Monetary Fund (IMF), the Government stated that it would eliminate the electricity subsidy to non-residential consumers by October 2009.

Figure I.9. Average residential prices, 1995–2008
(in dollars per kilowatt-hour)

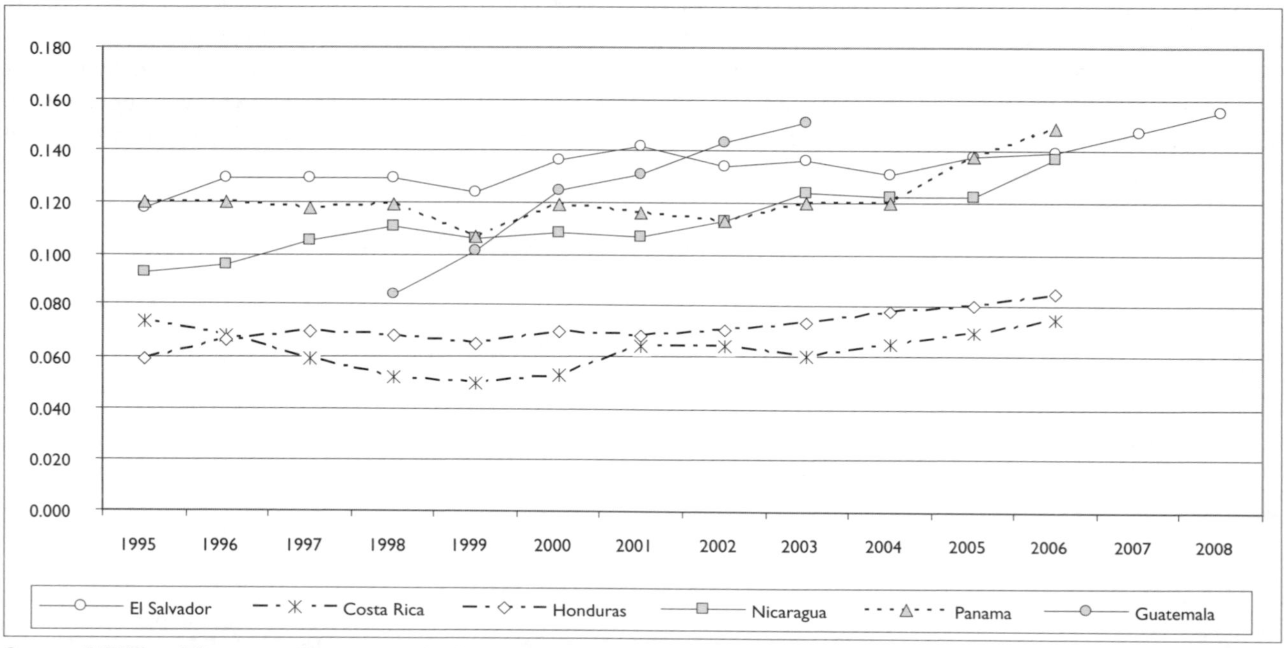

Sources: SIGET and Economic Commission for Latin America and the Caribbean.

In addition to boosting capacity and expanding the distribution network, the electricity sector has benefited from the presence of FDI through the social initiatives that some foreign companies have engaged in. One of the main foreign investors in the sector, AES, has paid particular attention to corporate social responsibility. The company has a campaign to educate and inform its consumers on the efficient and safe use of energy, explaining how to qualify for the government electricity subsidy and how to avoid accidents at home. Through their 25 offices nationwide, and partnering with local municipalities, AES distributes informational pamphlets and organizes activities to educate local communities on these issues. Furthermore,

---

[15] The other countries in the region that have privatized their electricity sector are: Guatemala, Nicaragua and Panama.

[16] El Salvador subsidizes residential users whose monthly consumption is less than 99 kWh. These consumers pay $0.07 per kilowatt-hour. Some 853,777 end-users benefited from this subsidy in 2008. This represents 60.6 per cent of all clients and 11.4 per cent of total demand of the entire distribution network, which, in turn, implies a monthly cost of $7.5 million to the Government.

through its four distributional companies, and in collaboration with FINET[17] and local governments, AES has so far been able to bring electricity to 23,000 new households.

Foreign investors are considering new projects that would diversify and expand El Salvador's sources of electricity, creating thousands of jobs and bringing more competitive prices to the market in the coming years. The most advanced project is the plan by AES to build the country's first coal-fired generation plant in La Unión, using clean-coal technology of the latest generation. Construction on the $600 million project could create 1,500 direct jobs. Once in operation, the 250 MW plant would employ 500 people.

6. FDI in telecommunications

The telecommunications sector has attracted $917 million of inflows in the past two decades. The sector also transitioned from being a state-owned monopoly to a competitive market with an important FDI presence. The monopoly of ANTEL was eliminated in 1997 and the enterprise split into two public companies: CTE was charged with the administration of fixed lines and infrastructure, and Intel took on mobile phone operations. A year later, 51 per cent of both companies was sold to foreign investors, marking the entrance of FDI in the sector; France Telecom paid $275 million to become CTE's majority shareholder, while Telefónica (Spain) paid $41 million for Intel. In 2003, France Telecom sold its CTE shares to América Móvil (Mexico) for $413 million. That same year, América Móvil bought the remaining stocks in the hands of the Government for $295 million to reach 94.4 per cent ownership.

As the incumbent in fixed telephony, CTE is the leader in a still highly concentrated market, with a 90 per cent market share. Telefónica, which bundles fixed-line with internet and cable television services, comes in second with a 3.5 per cent market share. Telemóvil, fully owned by Luxembourg-based Millicom, is in third place with 3.1 per cent, although its main operations are in mobile telephony where it is marketed under its Tigo brand. The market share of other companies is negligible, as they account for less than 5 per cent of the total.

Foreign investment in mobile telephony energized the market and introduced a high level of competition driven by technological innovation. There are three large operators with over 500,000 lines and close to 30 per cent of market share each, and also two more recent entrants that have made modest gains. Telemóvil was the first private company to provide cellular phone services in the country. Acquired by Millicom in the early 2000s, the company has been relegated from its position as market leader, partly because it was the last company to switch to GSM technology. Telefónica was the second company to enter the market after buying Intel in 1998, and it maintains its position. The third company to enter the market was CTE's mobile phone division Telecom Personal. Ever since América Móvil took over the company it has adopted an aggressive strategy to expand its operations, and it is currently the market leader with a 32 per cent market share.

Digicel (United States) mostly serves the Caribbean from its regional headquarters in Jamaica, but it has also spread out into Central America, and it began its operations in El Salvador in 2002. As a recent entrant, Digicel remains a minor player, although it has managed to secure close to 10 per cent of the market in a short period. Finally, Intelfon – a regional company with capital from El Salvador, Guatemala and Panama – was the first to introduce Motorola's iDEN technology that integrates digital radio communication to standard cellular communication, in late 2005. Intelfon markets mostly to corporate clients as a low-cost alternative.

Besides the private companies operating in fixed-line and mobile telephony, there are eleven *carriers*: companies that provide specialized services for international telecommunication. International calls administered by these companies account for more than $100 million in annual turnover.

---

[17] El Salvador's National Investment Fund for Electricity and Telecommunications

The last component in the ICT sector is the internet services that are provided by the main telephone companies. There has been a rapid migration away from dial-up to broadband service in recent years. The market for dial-up internet is dominated by two large suppliers: Telemóvil with almost 44 per cent of the market, and CTE with 37 per cent. The number of dial-up internet subscriptions peaked in 2003 at 93,395, but it fell dramatically to just over 1,000 by mid-2009, as dial-up was replaced by broadband internet. Meanwhile, the number of broadband subscriptions is steadily on the rise and reached 140,000 in mid-2009.

Telefónica was the pioneer in providing broadband internet in the country and maintains a privileged position with a market share of nearly 90 per cent. The fact that 99 per cent of internet users in El Salvador use fast internet with the latest technology is, in large part, attributed to FDI in the sector. Foreign investors have led the expansion of the fibre optics network in the country and have provided the know-how to administer the high-end technology. The installed fibre-optic network almost trebled in just six years, from 2,564km in 2003 to 7,162km in 2008.

The liberalization in telecommunications and the dominant role played by foreign investors have developed the sector into one of the most dynamic and fast-growing in the region. The number of fixed lines almost tripled in a decade, going from below 400,000 in 1998 to over 1.1 million by mid-2009. The number of fixed lines doubled in five years after FDI first entered the sector, something that took ANTEL 30 years to match before privatization. Growth in fixed lines was very high at first but since then has slowed significantly, partly due to the expansion in the use of mobile phones. El Salvador has experienced a boom in the number of mobile lines, which outstripped fixed lines as early as 2000. In the last decade, the number of mobile lines has increased from just over 100,000 in 1998 to more than 7 million by mid-2009. This dramatic growth places El Salvador as the leading country in Central America in terms of mobile lines per capita, with 113 phones per 100 people.

The quality of telecommunications services has dramatically improved with the presence of FDI. Most notably, the number of malfunctions in the telephone network reported by clients has declined since the year 2000, and the number of customer complaints has shown a declining trend since its peak in 2005. Likewise, the number of residential applications for a telephone line that have not been served has been reduced from over 170,000 in 1998 to just 577 in 2008. There is an improvement in most of the quality indicators reported by the Superintendencia General de Electricidad y Telecomunicaciones (SIGET) since its inception.

The impact that FDI has had on prices in fixed-line telephony has been threefold. Firstly, installation costs for fixed lines have fallen from $336 in 1998 to $53 currently. In addition, the waiting time for installation has declined markedly to a matter of days.

Secondly, the cost of making calls to the United States has diminished, notably due to the large demand in this market and the resulting competition between the 11 carrier companies. Since private carriers entered the market in 1998, the average cost of an international call to the United States has fallen from $0.80 to $0.23 per minute, with rates ranging from $0.018 to $0.37 in 2008, depending on the carrier, tariff plan and calling time.

Thirdly, there have been gradual increments in the costs of basic connection and of national calls per minute. The monthly basic connection charges for residential and commercial consumers increased slightly in the first few years following privatization and have stabilized at $8.3 and $14.2 respectively. The same is true of local and national call prices, which have stabilized at $0.023 and $0.040 per minute respectively

It is important to highlight, however, that before privatization the price of fixed telephone calls was well below the cost of supplying the service. Between 1980 and 1994, ANTEL kept a fixed rate which was not adjusted, even though cumulative inflation in that period was over 1,000 per cent. In 1995 and again in 1997,

ANTEL modified its rates, raising the costs of installation, calls per minute and access charges,[18] in order to make the sale of the state monopoly more attractive to investors.

Competition in mobile telephony has also led to a declining trend in the average price of calls per minute. When Telemóvil enjoyed a monopoly, the cost of a call from a mobile phone was $0.40 per minute. Currently, the cost of such a call can be as low as $0.05. Although there is a wide variety of subscription plans available, the cost of prepaid mobile-to-mobile telecommunication can be considered the most representative for the Salvadorean market, as it is the telecommunication service with the most demand: 86 per cent of mobile subscriptions are prepaid, and mobile-to-mobile accounts for 76 per cent of traffic in mobile telecommunication. The cost for this particular service ranges from $0.07 to $0.35 per minute.

Finally, thanks to the presence of competitive investors, the cost of internet services in El Salvador has declined too. The price for a monthly subscription of internet services averages about $22 and offers El Salvador the most competitive prices in the region.[19]

7.   FDI in maquilas and export processing zones (EPZs)

FDI in the maquilas represents a relatively modest proportion of total foreign investment in El Salvador, with cumulative flows of $425 million over the past two decades. In spite of this, maquilas are an important component of the manufacturing sector. Maquilas import intermediate goods for assembly or manufacturing and re-export the assembled product, in part back to the originating country. Most maquilas are located in export processing zones (EPZs) to benefit from duty-free treatment, since low trade costs are essential to the profitability of the industry.

There are 16 EPZs in El Salvador, representing a total of about 200 firms. According to the Fundación Salvadoreña para el Desarrollo Económico y Social (FUSADES), roughly 70 per cent of companies operating in EPZs are textile maquilas. Other assembly or manufacture companies are involved in paper (3 per cent), plastics (3 per cent), electronics (2 per cent) and chemicals (2 per cent). Garments and apparel represent 88 per cent of maquila exports. Besides the textile sector, other important products for exports are electrical appliances (7.9 per cent), together with some minor goods such as plastics (0.3 per cent), toys (0.2 per cent) and chemicals (0.2 per cent). Over 80 per cent of companies operating in EPZs are foreign-owned, many of them foreign affiliates of TNCs (e.g. Nike, Hanes, Lacoste). The main foreign investors in El Salvador's EPZs are from the United States (40 per cent), the Republic of Korea (14 per cent) and Taiwan Province of China (8 per cent).

Although textiles remain the predominant economic activity, there are signs that EPZs are attracting new types of companies in sectors such as health, energy and telecommunications. Motechi, for example, is a company that manufactures high-quality anatomical dental models. The German company has operated from El Progreso Free Zone since 1998. Soluciones Energéticas is a Salvadorean company that manufactures solar panels for export from the Santa Tecla Free Zone. These types of economic activities are more sophisticated and require high-skilled labour.

The maquila sector plays a key role in the country's trade balance. It has consistently been a net exporter, and its share of total exports has increased significantly over time, going from 19 per cent in 1991 and peaking at 60 per cent in 2003 before falling back to 42 per cent in 2008 (fig. 1.10). The United States is

---

[18] ANTEL's rates were revised in 1995 and 1997. The fixed-line cost of a call per minute was increased twice by 200 per cent, bringing it to nine times what it had been in 1994. The cost to establish the call, for residential and commercial users, was raised by 400 per cent in 1995, and then again by 86.7 per cent and 112 per cent respectively in 1997. Only the cost of international calls to the United States was reduced – by 50 per cent from $1.6 to $0.8 per minute.

[19] By comparison, the prices for monthly internet subscriptions in other Central American countries are: Costa Rica $26, Nicaragua $27, Honduras $33, Panama $39, Guatemala $53, according to 2006 World Bank estimates.

by far El Salvador's most important trading partner and this holds true for EPZs, as it is the destination for 87 per cent of their exports.

Figure I.10. Composition of exports, 1991–2008

(in millions of dollars)

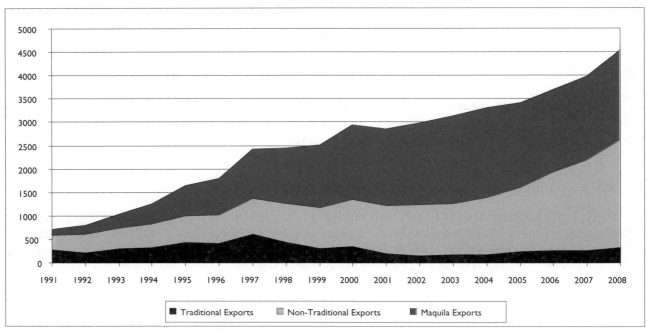

Source: BCR.

Net exports from maquilas have grown from $70.2 million in 1993 to $646.5 million in 2008. This suggests that the value addition that takes place in EPZs has increased as the maquilas produce more complex goods. However, net exports do not capture the vertical integration of local supply chains, because inputs from domestic suppliers to the EPZs are considered to be imports into the zone. Comparing the ratio of exports to imports across maquila industries in other countries, we can evaluate El Salvador's performance in terms of value addition. In this aspect, the Salvadorean maquila sector has improved in the past decades but does not perform as well as that of Costa Rica or the Dominican Republic, which suggests that there is room for higher value-addition processing to be carried out in El Salvador (fig. I.11).

The maquila sector and foreign investors in the EPZs have been an important engine for job creation in El Salvador. Employment in EPZs increased from 6,500 workers in 1991 to 50,000 in 1996. This represented 0.33 per cent and 2.1 per cent of the national workforce, respectively.[20] A more recent database developed by the International Labour Organization (ILO) estimates that around 76,000 workers were employed in EPZs in 2006. Including indirect employees, FUSADES calculates the number to be close to 94,000, or roughly 3 per cent of the labour force.

Employment in the maquila sector has a special potential for social development too, since, according to ILO estimates, 85 per cent of EPZ employees are women. The maquila sector is an important source of income for women and positively contributes to the welfare of low-income households.

Furthermore, working conditions and benefits in EPZs usually exceed those of domestic companies. A number of EPZs have developed on-site centres where workers can obtain free basic medical care. Although the main purpose is to avoid absenteeism, workers benefit from such services, and it takes some burden off

---

[20] Madani (1999).

the public health system. In addition, a number of EPZs also offer recreational facilities that are available to workers and their families outside of work hours.

Figure I.11. EPZs: ratio of exports to imports, 1991–2008

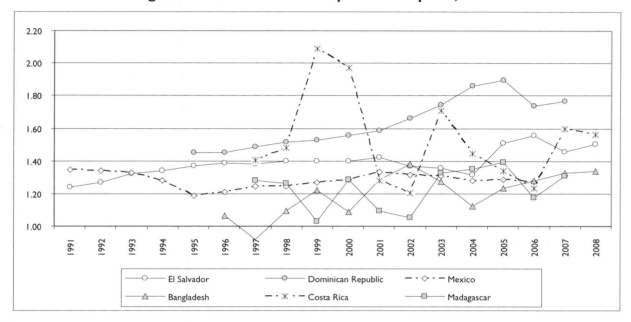

Sources: BCR and national central banks or EPZ authorities.

8. FDI in other sectors

Aside from the sectors discussed above, El Salvador has attracted FDI in other promising areas for growth, principally in services. This is the case with aeronautics, tourism, call centres and logistical services. Although they are all at different stages of development, these start-ups are further diversifying an already fairly evenly distributed national FDI portfolio and fit with El Salvador's aim of becoming a services-based economy.

Foreign investment in aeronautics is a well-known success in El Salvador. Established in 1982 to provide in-house maintenance for the Salvadorean airline TACA, Aeroman is a competitive aeronautic maintenance, repair and overhaul operator.[21] After receiving international certification by the Federal Aviation Administration (FAA) in 1998 and subsequently by the International Organization for Standardization (ISO) in 2003, Aeroman began to actively attract third-party clients. In late 2006, Air Canada's Technical Services acquired 80 per cent of Aeroman for $44.7 million, and it is planning on investing an additional $110 million to expand capacity from 4 to 16 hangars by 2016. At the moment, Aeroman has 1,500 employees and provides complete support services for the Airbus A320 series and the Boeing 737 and 757 series services for US Airways, JetBlue, Iberia, Aerolíneas Argentinas and Lloyd Aero Boliviano, among others.

Tourism is a sector that remains underdeveloped considering the country's potential, in some part due to the high levels of crime that persist in El Salvador. However, tourist arrivals have grown at double-digit levels in the past few years, reaching 1.9 million tourists in 2008.[22] Receipts from tourism have risen

---

[21] The maintenance, repair and overhaul market in Latin America was valued at $1.9 billion in 2007 and is expected to grow 5.3 per cent annually to reach $3.2 billion in the next decade. Moreover, almost 64 per cent of the North American airframe work is outsourced to third party providers and there is an increased outsourcing trend to Latin America that captured $51 million of the North American market in 2007.

[22] According to the Ministry of Tourism figures, tourist arrivals grew 15 per cent in 2006 and 2007, and 9 per cent in 2008.

too, from $373 million in 2003 to $941 million in 2007. In 2004, Decameron (Colombia) invested $9 million to acquire Club Salinitas and expanded the resort to 250 rooms. Today, the Royal Decameron Salinitas beach resort has 552 rooms and an estimated capital of $38 million. Besides being an important source of employment, the hotelier has been actively involved with the local community of Sonsonate, providing a daily meal to the schoolchildren from the Escuela Agueda and contributing to the remodelling of the school. Other major international chains present in El Salvador include Hilton, InterContinental, Marriot, Sheraton and Holiday Inn.

Although they do not represent a large portion of FDI stock, foreign investments in the offshore business services market have picked up in recent years. More and more "back office" work from developed countries is being outsourced to countries with more competitive labour costs, and El Salvador has been able to attract leading international companies such as Sykes, Dell and Stream to open call centres that offer customer and technical support.

Sykes, a world leader in business process outsourcing (BPO), entered El Salvador in 2003 with an investment of $8 million. Since then, it has had two expansions to its operations, in 2006 and 2008, representing an additional investment of almost $1.8 million; it currently employs 1,400 people. The computer manufacturer, Dell, opened a call centre in 2005 to cater to the Latin American and the United States markets. Dell's operations in El Salvador had over 1,500 employees until October 2008, when Stream Global Services acquired Dell's call centre in El Salvador.

A specialized type of BPO that has taken hold in El Salvador is that of logistical services. In April 2009, the Swedish company Wallenius Wilhelmsen Logistics, which specializes in automobile, heavy construction and agricultural machinery shipping, invested close to $1 million to open a data processing centre in the American Industrial Park EPZ. The centre keeps track of all shipments traffic between Latin America and the United States and Canada and manages receipts and payables. At the moment, the centre employs 30 people, but that number is expected to rise to 50 by the end of the year. There are several other foreign companies offering logistics services from El Salvador's EPZs – some with global scope like the German DHL, and others with a regional span such as CaribEx Worldwide, which specializes in warehousing and distribution.

C.   Assessment

As evidenced in this chapter, El Salvador has benefited from FDI in five key ways: (a) it has helped diversify the economy and generate employment; (b) it has contributed significantly to putting in place some of the infrastructure needed in a modern and competitive economy; (c) it has introduced novel industries using advanced technologies and new modes of production; (d) it has enhanced export capacity; and (e) it has been an important source of capital formation in a country with historically low levels of domestic saving. In other areas, including banking, the hopes and expectations of positive impact have probably not been completely fulfilled.

Foreign investment has allowed El Salvador to avail itself of niche opportunities in line with the country's comparative advantages that were not exploited previously as a consequence of a number of factors, including lack of venture capital, lack of expertise or lack of knowledge of international markets. In addition to establishing new streams of activities, foreign investors have also created a large number of jobs, not only in the export processing zones but also throughout the economy. As a result, they have also contributed to transferring skills and know-how to nationals. Foreign investments in the maquilas, in turn, have significantly boosted the export capacity of the country, and have helped El Salvador to avail itself of trade opportunities generated by concluding several free trade agreements.

El Salvador has been very successful in reforming the structure of the electricity and telecommunication sectors from vertically integrated public monopolies to disaggregated competitive structures led by private investment. This is a remarkable achievement, particularly in the electricity sector, where the regulatory complexities are high and where many developing countries have failed to achieve favourable outcomes. Adequate regulatory reforms and well-sequenced structural reforms have allowed El Salvador to attract significant amounts of FDI in electricity and telecommunications. Foreign investors currently dominate both sectors. They have increased the quality and availability of services to end-users (including electrification in rural areas), and in many cases provide services at a reduced cost, or at least at a regionally competitive price and under competitive market conditions. Foreign investment in both sectors has been sufficient to ensure the level of service needed by the economy, and has freed scarce government resources for investment in other infrastructure projects (e.g. roads) or in health and education, where public investment is more essential and cannot be (fully) substituted by private investment.

Although the benefits gained so far from FDI are substantial, El Salvador has the potential to perform significantly better still. Building on the experience of other small, open economies, El Salvador could attract higher flows of beneficial FDI. In particular, it should continue to use FDI to build and improve its infrastructure. As a small, open economy, El Salvador has no choice but to provide efficient and high-quality infrastructure services at regionally or globally competitive costs. These need to be the backbone of the competitiveness of locally established firms, and they are a key ingredient in attracting higher FDI inflows. As such, FDI can be used to attract FDI.

At the same time, El Salvador will need to confront the challenge of complying with WTO regulations on export subsidies, and therefore adjusting its fiscal regime in EPZs. It will also need to provide the general conditions necessary to attract niche investors and smaller TNCs, which may be less visible than the TNCs with global brands but may sometimes offer a better match for a small country such as El Salvador.

II. THE INVESTMENT FRAMEWORK

A. Introduction

El Salvador made a firm strategic and policy choice decades ago to pursue socio-economic development in an open and regulated market-economy setting. This choice is reflected in the regulatory framework for investment: El Salvador is widely open to FDI and well integrated in the regional and global trade community, and the adoption of the United States dollar as legal tender in 2001 cemented the country's integration in the world economy.

Successive governments have sought to firm the foundations for the development and strengthening of the economy through private initiative and investment, underpinned by an efficient and supportive public administration and public sector. Major reforms have been undertaken in this spirit in the past decade, including the privatization of important segments of the economy such as electricity, telecommunications, banking and pension funds. These operations were mostly successful as they were conducted in parallel with the establishment of appropriate sectoral regulations and the creation of strong oversight institutions.

A number of other reforms generated significant improvements in the business climate as El Salvador aimed to regulate its market economy efficiently, liberally and transparently, while imposing the lowest possible administrative burden on the private sector. Major reforms touched upon taxation, competition, consumer and environmental protection, sectoral regulations, international trade agreements and investment promotion.

The decision to pursue development in an open market-economy context, subjecting domestic operators to international competitive pressures, has yielded positive results. As a small country, this is probably the only option available for El Salvador to achieve its development goals, and it has been the strategic choice of all successful small countries around the world.[23]

Although foreign investors have already had a significant impact (chapter I), the FDI attraction potential remains partly untapped. As illustrated by the experience of other small economies, FDI could still contribute significantly more to development.[24]

In order to accelerate progress towards the achievement of its development goals, maximize the contribution of FDI in this respect, and manage the implications of the global financial and economic crisis, El Salvador will need to step up its efforts to create a highly efficient and effective regulatory framework for investment. This chapter provides concrete recommendations on the areas of the framework that deserve the most attention over the coming years, not only as they pertain to FDI, but also as they affect national investors.

B. Entry, establishment, treatment and protection of FDI

El Salvador has long adopted an open attitude towards FDI with a high standard of protection. The Law on Investment[25] explicitly stipulates that it seeks to encourage investment – and FDI in particular – in order to contribute to socio-economic development through increased productivity, job creation, exports and diversification. This intention is effectively translated into a modern investment law that addresses the key concerns of foreign investors.

---

[23] Small OECD economies (with a population of less than 10 million people) have all long been globalized economically and are among the wealthiest countries in the world (e.g. Austria, Denmark, Finland, New Zealand, Norway and Switzerland). The most successful small countries in transition (Croatia, Estonia, Latvia, Lithuania and Slovenia) have also adopted an open market-economy model. Singapore and Hong Kong (China) are other striking examples.

[24] UNCTAD (forthcoming, a) draws policy lessons on FDI attraction in small countries from the experience of Estonia and Jamaica.

[25] Ley de Inversiones.

1. FDI entry and establishment

FDI entry restrictions are limited in scope and mostly transparent. The Law on Investment stipulates, as a general principle, that any natural or legal person is entitled to make investments of any nature in El Salvador, irrespective of nationality, residence or other characteristics. This is obviously subject to certain limitations set by law.

The Law on Investment itself defines a short list of constraints on investors, many of which are not FDI entry restrictions as such, but rather operational requirements applicable to all investors.[26] Two general entry restrictions are nevertheless set in the law:

- Small businesses in commerce, industry and services are reserved to Salvadorean and Central American citizens.[27] This restriction is also established in the Constitution. Its application is nevertheless clouded by some vagueness, as a precise definition of small businesses is not provided in the law or regulations. There are also indications that the restriction is not applied, particularly since the 2008 reform of the commercial code lowered the minimum capital of limited liability companies to $2,000.

  The central bank (BCR), the ministry of the economy and the finance ministry (Hacienda) have all adopted slightly different definitions of "small businesses" for their own purposes. The BCR ranks all companies with annual sales of below $685,714 (6 million colones) and with fewer than 50 employees as micro or small enterprises, while the ministry of the economy only applies the employees criterion.

  El Salvador's schedule of specific commitments under the WTO's General Agreement on Trade in Services (GATS) specifies that the country will apply the small business restriction on a horizontal basis (i.e. all activities of industry, commerce and services) and that the amounts to qualify as a small business will be set by law. Annex I (schedule of El Salvador) of the United States–Dominican Republic–Central American Free Trade Agreement (CAFTA-DR), in turn, explicitly stipulates that the small enterprise FDI entry restriction applies for companies with a capitalization of less than $200,000.

- Foreign ownership of rural land and assets is subject to a reciprocity clause with the country of origin of the investor.[28] El Salvador also imposes a general cap of 245 hectares on ownership of rural land by a single entity. However, this cap applies to nationals as well as foreigners (section C.8).

Aside from these restrictions defined in the Law on Investment, a number of sector-specific laws and regulations contain limitations on FDI entry. These restrictions are limited and well contained, however, and consist mainly of the following:

- A minimum of 51 per cent of locally incorporated banks must be owned by: (i) Salvadorean or Central American citizens; (ii) locally incorporated companies owned by Salvadoreans or Central Americans; (iii) Central American banks from countries with adequate prudential regulations; and (iv) banks and financial institutions from anywhere in the world as long as their country of residence applies prudential regulations in conformity with international standards and if the institution is ranked as "first class" by rating agencies of international renown. The latter provision effectively opens up the banking system to full foreign ownership.

---

[26] This includes the stipulation that mineral resources can only be exploited through concessions, that public services may be subject to price controls even when supplied by private operators, and that concessions are required to exploit loading bays, railroads or canals.

[27] Costa Rica, Guatemala, Honduras and Nicaragua.

[28] This restriction does not apply if rural land is acquired for industrial purposes.

- Licences for television and radio broadcasting may be granted only to Salvadorean citizens or locally incorporated companies whose capital is owned by Salvadoreans at the rate of at least 51 per cent.

- Passenger transport by road within El Salvador may only be operated by Salvadorean nationals. Road transport of goods within the country, in turn, is subject to the same 51 per cent rule as above.

- As is customary in all countries, El Salvador imposes constraints on the exercise of certain professional services by foreign nationals, including as a result of issues of recognition of degrees and qualifications and citizenship/residence requirements. In some cases, Central American citizens benefit from a more favourable treatment than other foreigners do. The most important professions affected include construction, architecture and engineering, public accounting and auditing, notaries and health services.

The Law on Investment created the National Office of Investments (Oficina Nacional de Inversiones (ONI)) under the Ministry of the Economy, in order to "facilitate, centralize and coordinate" the establishment procedures set by law. It was designed not only as a single window to facilitate investment by nationals and foreigners, but also as data collection mechanism.

According to the Law on Investment, foreign investors *must* register their investments with the ONI. It is also explicitly specified, however, that registration may not be conditional upon performance or operational requisites, such as local content or export requirements. In addition to conducting foreign investment registration, the ONI was also structured to facilitate the whole establishment process. A number of administrative services are thus represented at the ONI.

In spite of the legal requirement and the facilitation services offered, many foreign investors do not register their investment with the ONI. There appear to be no legal implications to this, as registration is not a condition for gaining special treatment or incentives, and no sanction is applied for failing to register. In addition, foreign investors are able to proceed with all standard company establishment procedures without the ONI registration.

These establishment procedures – which can be conducted at the ONI – are processed at the National Registry Centre (Centro Nacional de Registros (CNR)) under a single-window service (trámite integral). The procedures have been simplified over the past decade, and investors are now able to incorporate their company, obtain their tax identification number, and register with the social security institute as an employer at the CNR. In addition, El Salvador has been a leader in the region in its use of e-governance (box II.1).

2.   FDI treatment and protection

El Salvador provides a high standard of treatment and protection to all foreign investors under the Law on Investment. It further consolidated and increased this standard for investors from Costa Rica, the Dominican Republic, Guatemala, Honduras, Nicaragua and the United States under the investment chapter of CAFTA-DR. In addition, El Salvador has signed 24 bilateral investment treaties (BITs) with major home countries for FDI.

a.   General standard of treatment and protection

The Law on Investment stipulates that foreign investors have the "same rights and obligations" as national investors and that discriminatory measures to hinder their establishment or the administration,

---

Box II.1. E-governance in El Salvador

El Salvador has long emphasized the use of information technology (IT) tools to modernize public administration and services. A number of programmes have been launched in the past decade, including "e-país", focused on the use of IT tools, and "El Salvador Eficiente", focused on simplifying administrative procedures. The strategy has put around 800 services online in 54 public institutions. Some of the most relevant e-governance tools include:

- **e-CNR** (http://www.e.cnr.gob.sv/portal): The CNR has put online a catalogue of its services, together with the required forms and instructions. The absence of a law on electronic signatures means that it is not yet possible to complete the administrative procedures online, but the system is capacitated to do so and should be available once a legal framework on e-signatures is adopted. The e-CNR can also be used to provide notifications to petitioners on the status of their procedures (via SMS or e-mail). Among other things, the e-CNR covers procedures related to company registration, intellectual property, and land and mortgages registry.

- **Trade facilitation**: The customs office (http://www.aduana.gob.sv) has stepped up its efforts to use IT tools to facilitate trade in recent years. In addition to providing comprehensive online information on import duties and procedures (a requirement under CAFTA-DR), the office is making increasing use of electronic submission and processing of import documents. Certain categories of importers are already able to track their cargo online (section C.4).

- In addition, the Ministry of Agriculture (http://www.mag.gob.sv) and the Ministry of Health (http://www.gaisa-mspas.gob.sv) provide online services to issue phytosanitary permits for the import of food, beverages and live animals. The eSalPort website (http://www.esalport.gob.sv) allows importers and exporters to track their cargo or shipments.

- **e-regulations** (http://elsalvador.e-regulations.org): This project, implemented with UNCTAD's technical assistance, offers step-by-step information and guidance for investors wishing to create a company, buy land, legalize documents or trade goods.

- **Electronic payments**: the P@GOES system was established to allow investors or individuals to pay taxes and fees for government services.

Sources: UNCTAD and institutional websites.

---

use, extension, sale or liquidation of their investments are prohibited.[29] El Salvador applies a strict definition of national treatment that does not allow more favourable treatment or special incentives to be granted to foreign investors only. Although the most favoured nation (MFN) principle is not explicitly mentioned in the law, its article 7 prevents discrimination on the basis of the nationality or residence of the investor. The law also forbids specific performance requirements on foreign investors, such as those linked to export, local content or technological transfers.

A wide definition of "investment" is used in the law, which covers tangible and intangible goods and flows of capital aimed at executing economic activities for the purpose of producing goods or services. The transfer of funds related to the investment is subject to strong and wide legal guarantees that cover, among other things: (a) profits and dividends; (b) loan and interest payments; (c) proceeds from the sale, liquidation or expropriation of assets; and (d) any payment resulting from legal activities related to the investment.

---

[29] These principles are naturally subject to the proviso of restrictions that may be applied by law on the entry of foreign investors or on the extent of their participation in certain sectors.

These guarantees on the transfer of funds were further solidified by the adoption of the United States dollar as legal tender in 2001 (section C.5).

Private property rights – including intellectual property rights – are recognized and guaranteed by the Constitution, which also stipulates that the State must promote and protect private initiative in order to promote wealth creation and wide benefits for the population. The Constitution also conditions expropriations on a duly justified public purpose or social interest and pending previous and fair compensation. Under certain circumstances, compensation (e.g. for the construction of water, electricity or road infrastructure) may occur ex post. When the amount justifies it, the Constitution also allows compensation to be paid by instalments over a period of up to 15 years, subject to interest payments.

The Law on Expropriations[30] regulates more precisely the conditions under which expropriations may occur. It provides a relatively wide definition of public purpose, as defined in three main categories: (a) works needed to provide public services (e.g. roads, water, railway, electricity, cemeteries, prisons or schools); (b) patents may be declared of public purpose if the invention can create substantial national wealth or contribute to public defence and if the owner refuses to grant a licence in El Salvador; and (c) public purpose may be declared in order to exploit minerals.

The determination of public purpose must follow due process through the court of first instance, except for the construction of road infrastructure, in which case the law allows the Ministry of Transport to proceed by executive order. The parties must first seek mutual agreement on the compensation. If no agreement can be found, compensation is determined by a panel of experts through a judicial procedure. In the case of disagreements between the experts, the value of the land and buildings as stated in the tax declaration may be used as the basis for compensation.

Foreign investors have access to domestic courts under the same terms as national investors and are not subject to any discrimination. The effectiveness of the judicial system, however, remains an important weakness in El Salvador, particularly in terms of commercial justice. The Law on Investment allows foreign investors to submit disputes with the State to international conciliation or arbitration under the International Centre for Settlement of Investment Disputes (ICSID). El Salvador does not require the exhaustion of local administrative or judicial remedies as a condition for its consent to recourse to ICSID, which is granted by law. In addition, El Salvador allows investors originating from states that are not members of ICSID to access its conciliation and arbitration mechanism through the ICSID Additional Facility.

The enforcement of international arbitration awards is facilitated by El Salvador's membership of the Convention on the Recognition and Enforcement of Foreign Arbitral Awards (New York Convention). To date, only three cases have been referred to ICSID: (a) Commerce Group Corp. and San Sebastián Gold Mines filed a case in August 2009; (b) Pacific Rim Cayman filed a case in June 2009 asking for damages in the hundreds of millions of dollars as a result of claimed unjustified delays in granting gold mining rights following previous exploration work; and (c) Inceysa Vallisoletana (motor vehicle inspection) filed a claim in 2003, which was dismissed for lack of jurisdiction by ICSID.[31] A fourth case, regarding interests in the geothermal company LaGeo, has been filed by Italian electricity firm ENEL to the International Chamber of Commerce.

b.   Investment chapter of CAFTA-DR

Chapter 10 of CAFTA-DR provides an even stronger standard of treatment and protection to investors from Costa Rica, the Dominican Republic, Guatemala, Honduras, Nicaragua and the United States – a standard that Salvadorean investors also benefit from in those countries. To begin with, investment is defined

---

[30] Ley de Expropiación y de Ocupación de Bienes por el Estado.
[31] The arbitration tribunal determined that its jurisdiction did not extend to investments that were made fraudulently.

even more widely than in the Law on Investment to include – among other things – all shares, stocks and other forms of equity participation in a company, bonds and loans, futures, options and other derivatives, and intellectual property rights. The protection accorded under chapter 10 thus covers a wide range of assets, which go beyond FDI *stricto sensu*.[32]

The main issues covered in chapter 10 are the following:

- **National treatment** is provided and defined as treatment no less favourable than that accorded to national investors in like circumstances, with respect to the establishment, acquisition, expansion, management, conduct, operation and sale or other disposition of investments;

- **MFN treatment** is defined as treatment no less favourable than that accorded to investors from any other State;

- The **minimum standard of treatment** must cover fair and equitable treatment and full protection and security. Customary international law is specifically mentioned as a benchmark on minimum standard of treatment;

- Protection against **expropriation** is significantly stronger under CAFTA-DR than under national law, and the Constitution contains provisions that are not aligned with these commitments. In particular, CAFTA-DR is more protective of investors in terms of compensation, which must be "prompt, adequate and effective", paid without delay and be equivalent to the fair market value of the expropriated asset immediately before the expropriation is announced;

- **Transfer rights** are defined similarly, as under the Law on Investment. The ban on **performance requirements** is stricter, as the agreement prohibits conditioning the receipt of investment incentives or advantages on compliance with certain operational requirements;

- **Investor–State dispute settlement** is subject to very comprehensive treatment in chapter 10. Each CAFTA-DR party grants its automatic consent to investors from the other parties to have recourse to international conciliation or arbitration if they elect to do so, either under ICSID or under the United Nations Commission on International Trade Law (UNCITRAL) arbitration rules. In addition, chapter 10 contains detailed provisions on the selection of arbitrators, the conduct of arbitration, governing law, and the enforcement of awards.

c.   Network of bilateral investment treaties

El Salvador started negotiating bilateral investment treaties in the early 1990s. By 2009, 20 BITs had entered into force and an additional four were pending ratification. In addition, all its free trade agreements contain investment provisions.[33] These BITs or investment provisions of trade agreements cover the majority of the large source countries of FDI in El Salvador.

The BITs contain relatively standard dispositions. Most make investment promotion an explicit goal of the treaty, in addition to ensuring fair treatment and protection. In general, BITs provide national, MFN and fair and equitable treatment, guarantee transfer rights, provide access to international arbitration under ICSID or UNCITRAL, and protect against expropriation. As is the case for CAFTA-DR, the key area

---

[32] UNCTAD (forthcoming, e) discusses the development implications of the use of wide-ranging definitions of "investment" in international investment agreements. It warns developing countries about the need to grasp fully the implications of offering protection to non-FDI investments under bilateral investment treaties. It also attempts to offer a more narrow and development-oriented definition of "investment" for consideration in future bilateral investment treaties.

[33] Including under CAFTA-DR and treaties with Chile, Mexico, Panama and Taiwan Province of China.

where protection is stronger under the provisions of the BITs than under domestic laws is in the case of expropriations.

3.   Recommendations on FDI entry, establishment, treatment and protection

El Salvador's decision to centre its development strategy around a small open-economy model is reflected in its legislation regarding foreign direct investment. The framework is open, favourable, non-discriminatory, and protective towards FDI. In addition, a number of international commitments further solidify this enabling framework. A few clarifications or adaptations could nevertheless bring additional credibility and benefits to El Salvador and further promote FDI:

- The protection of small national businesses from FDI needs to be clarified and better defined by law. It is important to ensure that potentially valuable, but initially small, foreign investments are not impeded. A restriction based on capital invested as defined under CAFTA-DR is not the best way to protect small businesses, as it runs the risk of nipping in the bud small start-up foreign investments in potentially new and high-growth sectors.[34] A more fine-tuned approach to protecting small businesses in sensitive sectors is possible and desirable. It should be based on precisely defined sectors, and allow for exceptions.

- Registration with the ONI has proved ineffective and is not strictly enforced. As it stands, it serves little purpose and does not really help El Salvador collect statistics on FDI flows. Instead, a more flexible and survey-based approach to collecting data on investment could be put in place, both for foreign and national investments.[35] The facilitation services offered by the ONI could be integrated into the CNR, which would then become the single point of entry and one-stop shop for all investors setting up their businesses.

- It would be valuable for El Salvador to further promote and facilitate the mobility of professionals, at least among Central American countries. More details on this issue are provided in section C.7.

- The Constitution and the Law on Expropriation contain provisions on expropriations that are not aligned with El Salvador's commitments under CAFTA-DR and its BITs. This situation ought to be remedied, in order to reflect international best practices on expropriations that El Salvador seems to have largely endorsed. This would provide greater certainty to all investors, regardless of their nationality, and would avoid inconsistencies between domestic law and international commitments.

- El Salvador has had to deal with three cases referred to ICSID thus far, including two only very recently. Given its policy of allowing investor-State disputes to be brought to international arbitration at the investor's discretion, and given the legal costs involved (box II.2), it would be worthwhile for El Salvador to establish mechanisms to avoid such recourse as much as possible. It is also important that El Salvador be better prepared institutionally to handle such cases if and when they occur. UNCTAD (forthcoming, d) considers the alternatives to arbitration in international investment agreements. It also suggests dispute prevention policies, building on international experiences and good practices.

---

[34] One must bear in mind how small Google, Hewlett-Packard, Microsoft or Wal-Mart were at their beginnings.
[35] UNCTAD provides technical assistance in this area. UNCTAD (2009e, f, g) provide training manuals on data collection.

Box II.2. International arbitration under ICSID

A total of 301 cases have been brought to international arbitration under ICSID since the entry into force of the Washington Convention in 1966. The first case was filed in 1972 by Holiday Inn and others, against Morocco. Until the late 1990s, few cases were registered with ICSID, typically two or three per year. There has been a sharp increase in the number of cases since 1997, however, with a peak of 37 in 2007 (fig. II.1).

Figure II.1. Cases registered with ICSID, 1972–2009

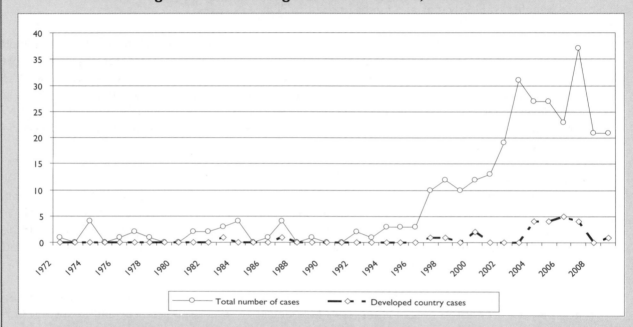

The vast majority of cases have been filed against governments in developing countries or economies in transition. Out of 301 cases, only 24 involved developed countries. ICSID charges $25,000 for lodging a request, in addition to a $20,000 annual administrative charge. Arbitrators are paid a fee of $3,000 per day of meeting or work performed in connection with the proceedings, in addition to reimbursement of expenses. By far the largest costs incurred in international arbitration, however, are legal assistance fees, which can amount to several million dollars.

Unlike in commercial arbitration cases, parties involved in investment arbitration have usually had to bear their full legal costs, while sharing equally the costs of arbitration. As a result, the costs involved in ICSID arbitration may be very high for the governments of developing countries, even if the investors lose their cases. It must be noted, however, that there have been some cases in recent years where the arbitration tribunal has at least partly applied the "loser pays" principle.[36]

Source: ICSID.

---

[36] This was the case in EDF Services Ltd. vs. Romania, where the arbitration tribunal ordered EDF to contribute $6 million to the costs of the Government of Romania, while the arbitration costs were shared equally. The tribunal referred to precedents under NAFTA/UNCITRAL where the arbitration tribunal had at least partly applied the "loser pays" principle in investment cases.

C. General measures for regulating business

1. Taxation

El Salvador will be confronted with two key tax policy challenges in the years to come. On the one hand, it will have to eliminate the export processing zones (EPZ) incentives that are not compatible with the Agreement on Subsidies and Countervailing Measures of the WTO rules. On the other hand, it will have to gradually increase government revenues as a share of GDP, in order to provide the administrative and public services (e.g. core infrastructure, education, health) needed by an aspiring upper middle-income country. In 2008, central government revenues and grants represented only 14.6 per cent of GDP (table II.1). Although this is comparable to Costa Rica and is higher than in Guatemala, it remains below Mexico or Panama, and well short of more advanced countries such as Brazil or Chile.[37]

Table II.1. Central government revenues
(per cent of GDP)

	2004	2005	2006	2007	2008
Tax revenues (net)	11.5	12.5	13.3	13.4	13.0
Income tax (net)	3.4	3.9	4.2	4.6	4.5
Import duties	1.1	1.1	1.1	1.0	0.8
VAT (net)	6.0	6.5	7.0	6.8	6.6
Non-tax revenues	1.7	1.0	1.1	1.2	1.6
Memorandum: Refunds	-0.7	-0.6	-0.5	-0.7	-0.9

Sources: Banco Central de Reserva de El Salvador.

Like many countries in the world, El Salvador has used corporate tax policy to foster investment and promote FDI. Unlike others, however, it has managed to preserve a relatively straightforward tax regime with a reasonably simple incentives structure, centred around the EPZ regime and the special treatment granted to exporters of services. In spite of this, El Salvador ranks a poor 154th and 127th out of 181 countries in the World Bank's 2009 *Doing Business* rankings on the number of tax payments and time spent to comply.[38] The sections below assess the current tax regime. Based on the weaknesses, challenges and needs highlighted above, a number of recommendations are provided, with a view to putting in place a tax regime that both encourages investments in a non-distortive fashion and allows the Government to generate sufficient revenues.

a. Corporate income taxation

The Law on Income Tax[39] was overhauled in 1991 and has subsequently been subject to various amendments to further simplify the tax code. A number of principles and objectives are stated in the preamble, including simplicity, ease of procedures, transparency, neutrality, certainty, a moderate tax burden, and a widening of the tax base through a reduction in exemptions and rebates. El Salvador has upheld several of these objectives, but problems remain both in terms of tax structure and administration.

A fiscal reform was also adopted by the National Assembly in December 2009. The amendments to various laws (including the Law on Income Tax and the Law on Value-Added Tax) did not affect the structure of corporate taxation. A number of rules were introduced or tightened in respect of exempt income and

---

[37] The levels are as follows: Brazil, 38.2 per cent (2007); Chile, 29.5 per cent (2007); Costa Rica, 15.5 per cent (2008); Guatemala, 12.1 per cent (2008); Mexico, 16.9 per cent (2008); and Panama, 19.5 per cent (2007).

[38] On the assessment of the financial burden of taxes, El Salvador ranks significantly better in 54th position. A comparative analysis of the burden of corporate taxation using UNCTAD's methodology is provided below.

[39] Ley de Impuesto sobre la Renta.

deductions from taxable income. The main objectives are to limit tax evasion and tax engineering, including through transactions with tax havens or through transfer pricing. The fiscal reform also affects excises and duties on goods such as alcoholic beverages, tobacco or fuels.

Corporate income is subject to a standard tax rate of 25 per cent, while capital gains are taxed at 10 per cent. Companies are taxed on a territorial basis, and all standard deductions are allowed in determining taxable income. Depreciation rates for tax purposes are set by the companies, subject to certain caps, including: (a) 5 per cent for buildings; (b) 20 per cent for machinery; (c) 25 per cent for vehicles; (d) 25 per cent for software; and (e) 50 per cent for other movable assets. Depreciation for tax purposes must be done on a straight-line basis and at a unique rate for the whole duration of the depreciation.

Contrary to common worldwide practice, El Salvador does not allow companies to carry forward their losses.[40] In addition, companies are not allowed to programme depreciation of fixed assets over time (for example by deferring deductions from one year to another) in order to ensure that asset depreciation has a genuine effect on the income tax base. This double constraint means that companies cannot avail themselves of the tax relief from investment and expansion that they expect and obtain in most countries. As such, it acts as a disincentive to investment and puts El Salvador in an uncompetitive position.

In another departure from common worldwide practice, El Salvador imposes monthly advance payments on corporate income taxes, equivalent to 1.5 per cent of turnover. These payments are credited towards the corporate income tax due at the end of the fiscal year. Excess payments may be refunded, imputed on other income tax obligations, or credited towards future monthly advance payments. While such advance payments are common, most countries impose them on a quarterly or semi-annual basis. Many countries also impose advance payments on the basis of self-assessments of taxable income, not as a percentage of turnover.

Monthly advance payments can represent an important call on the cash flow of companies, particularly the most dynamic ones. They also represent a heavy administrative burden for investors and the tax authorities alike, both as a result of the monthly payments and the refunds due on the closing of the tax year. In 2008, refunds on income tax represented almost $50 million, or 0.2 per cent of GDP. This figure is likely to underestimate excess payments, as companies can also elect to credit the closing annual balance towards future monthly dues. The administrative burden of these monthly payments is one of the reasons why El Salvador ranks poorly on the *Doing Business* rankings on the number of tax payments and the time spent to comply. They also run counter to the principle of "ease of procedures" as stated in the law.

El Salvador does not tax dividends, whether distributed to nationals or foreigners, as long as the company has duly paid income taxes on the underlying profits. Other payments to non-residents (royalties, interest payments, service fees) are subject to a withholding tax of 20 per cent. Capital gains are taxed at 10 per cent, with the possibility of deducting capital losses on other operations going back five years at most.

The double taxation treaty (DTT) with Spain, ratified in September 2008, is El Salvador's first and only DTT to date.[41] It allows the parties to apply withholding taxes on dividends at a maximum rate of 12 per cent and to tax other payments (interest, royalties, fees) at up to 10 per cent. At the moment, the territorial base of taxation protects Salvadorean companies investing abroad from double taxation, and the absence of dividend withholding tax shelters foreign companies in El Salvador. Nevertheless, the absence of a DTT network penalizes foreign investors in El Salvador, as they may be subject to double taxation on intra-company interest payments and royalties. As of mid-2009, preliminary negotiations on DTTs had started with Chile, Qatar and the United States.

---

[40] Many countries in the world allow unlimited loss carry-forward. Those that do not, typically, have a provision allowing a three-year or five-year loss carry-forward. There are few countries that do not allow any loss carry-forward like El Salvador.

[41] The Treaty has been ratified by El Salvador, but not yet by Spain.

El Salvador has a relatively straightforward system of investment incentives, which are provided by five laws: (a) the Law on Industrial and Commercial Free Zones; (b) the Law on International Services; (c) the Law on Export Reactivation; (d) the Law on Industrial Development; and (e) the Law on Tourism.[42] The largest incentives are related to export performance and are granted under the first two laws.

El Salvador has put in place a modern EPZ regime that encourages the participation of private investors as zone developers and managers by providing them with similar incentives to those granted to companies operating in the zones. As of mid-2009, El Salvador had 16 EPZs, most privately owned and run, in which more than 200 companies operate (chapter I). Most industrial and manufacturing operations are allowed to establish in EPZs, with a few exceptions as specified by law.[43] Companies established in the zones must be export-oriented but are allowed to sell some of their output on the Salvadorean market, subject to the payment of import duties, value-added tax (VAT) and corporate income tax on the corresponding operations.

The incentives provided under the Law on Industrial and Commercial Free Zones are extremely generous and consist of: (a) full and indefinite exemption on corporate income tax and municipal taxes; and (b) exemption from all duties and VAT on the import of equipment, machinery, raw materials and intermediate goods used for production.

The Law on International Services was adopted in 2007 to provide the same incentives to exporters of services. It is more restrictive, however, as it delimits the services that are eligible for incentives and imposes specific eligibility conditions. The eligible services are: (a) international distribution and logistics; (b) call centres; (c) IT services (software development); (d) research and development; (e) aircraft and boat maintenance; (f) business process outsourcing; (g) medical services; and (h) international financial services.

The law requires some of these services to be provided from "services parks" similar to EPZs, while others, such as call centres and maintenance operations, can be operated as individual units outside of the parks. As for EPZs, El Salvador wishes the private sector to lead the development and management of services parks. Developers are thus granted similar incentives to those provided to companies operating in the parks. As is the case for companies operating under the EPZ regime, services providers are allowed to sell to the local market, subject to the payment of all applicable taxes and duties.

In addition, the law imposes a number of conditions to benefit from the special tax regime. International distribution and logistics companies must have warehouses of at least 500m^2. BPO companies must invest at least $150,000 in the first year, create 10 permanent jobs and have a contract of a minimum of one year with a client. Medical services providers must invest a minimum of $10 million ($3 million if surgery services are not offered) and must be established outside of the San Salvador metropolitan area and departmental capitals.

The incentives provided by the other three laws are more limited. Under the Law on Export Reactivation, exporters of goods and services outside Central America benefit from a non-taxable refund equivalent to 6 per cent of the FOB value of the export. All exports are eligible, with the exception of mining and traditional products (coffee, cotton and sugar).

The Law on Industrial Development offers duty-free imports of capital goods and inputs and grants temporary exemptions or reductions on corporate income taxes. Incentives are restricted to "pioneering" projects or "necessary" industries,[44] and companies must be 50 per cent Salvadorean-owned to be eligible. The incentives under the Law on Industrial Development have not been used extensively lately.

---

[42] (a) Ley de Zonas Francas Industriales y de Comercialización; (b) Ley de Servicios Internacionales; (c) Ley de Reactivación de las Exportaciones; (d) Ley de Fomento Industrial; and (e) Ley de Turismo.

[43] These include the production and commercialization of cement, sugar or alcohol.

[44] They are defined as those that produce goods or services to satisfy the basic needs of the population (e.g. food, health and housing).

The Law on Tourism grants a 10-year exemption on corporate income taxes and a 5-year reduction of up to 50 per cent on municipal taxes. This incentive is granted for projects in excess of $50,000, on the condition that they be declared of "national touristic interest" by the Ministry of Tourism. These incentives were aimed at kick-starting the sector and are granted for a transition period of five years, which will run until the end of 2010. Beneficiary companies are also required to make a contribution of 5 per cent of net income to a tourism development fund during the exoneration period.

In 2005, El Salvador established a four-year trust fund to provide direct financial support to investors in strategic sectors in order to help them establish in the country (Fideicomiso Especial para la Creación de Empleo en Sectores Productivos Estratégicos (FECEPE)). The fund aimed to compensate investors for positive localization externalities and the training of workers. Eligibility conditions included the creation of a minimum of 250 permanent jobs with an average monthly wage of at least $200. Beneficiaries also had to commit to maintaining the investment and jobs for a minimum period of time, except in cases of force majeure.

Close to $40 million of direct financial support were provided to 15 companies between 2005 and 2009. Although this type of support/subsidies is not uncommon, including in OECD economies, it is highly questionable whether the costs have been justifiable in relation to the long-term benefits. As the experience of many countries shows, direct subsidies to private investors frequently fail to promote sustainable investments and job creation in the long run. In addition, positive externalities are often hard to quantify, which makes a cost/benefit analysis very difficult. It is likely that public funds of the order of magnitude of those spent under the FECEPE would be better invested in long-term infrastructure projects benefiting the economy as a whole, such as – for example – the development of a private–public partnership to make the port of La Unión operational (chapter III).

A comparative assessment shows that El Salvador's general regime imposes an overall corporate tax burden that is mostly on a par with or lighter than regional comparators, depending on the sector (annex I). Similarly to most other countries in the region, the EPZ regime is extremely favourable to investors as it provides a virtually full tax exemption. In that sense, El Salvador does not differentiate itself from its neighbours.

b. Value-added tax

Value-added tax was introduced in 1992 to replace stamp duty on invoices. The system is modern and well administered, and VAT is the largest source of tax revenue, at close to 7 per cent of GDP, well ahead of income taxes. All companies are subject to VAT, regardless of size or turnover.

El Salvador applies a standard input-output VAT method with monthly returns. The standard rate that applies to the majority of goods and services is 13 per cent. Exports of goods and services are zero-rated, while a number of services are exempt.[45] Exporters have the option to either obtain refunds on excess VAT payments or to impute against other tax obligations. The system of refunds appears to function well, and the administration is legally obliged to process refunds within 30 business days. In 2008, VAT refunds to exporters amounted to 0.7 per cent of GDP. Companies that do not export, on the other hand, may not obtain refunds and are restricted to compensating excess payments against future VAT obligations.

c. Customs duties

El Salvador has significantly reduced its level of tariff protection, as part of its open-economy development strategy and to submit domestic companies to international competitive pressure. Under the

---

[45] These include health, education, public transport, personal insurance and water supply.

Central American Common Market (CACM), established in 1960, El Salvador applies a common external tariff of 0 or 5 per cent for capital goods and raw materials; 10 per cent for intermediate goods; and 15 per cent for consumption goods.

Most trade between CACM partners (Costa Rica, El Salvador, Guatemala, Honduras and Nicaragua) is entirely free of duties, with a few exceptions, particularly for agricultural products. In addition, El Salvador has joined a number of free trade agreements with its historic trading partners – in particular CAFTA-DR, but also including Chile, Mexico and Taiwan Province of China. Although all of these agreements have a gradual tariff-elimination schedule on certain sensitive goods, they have significantly reduced the level of effective protection enjoyed by domestic producers (section C.2).

The trade opening policy means that import duties fell from 2.1 per cent of GDP in 1995 to 0.8 per cent in 2008. This is equivalent to less than 6 per cent of total government revenue and indicates that El Salvador has definitively given up on the use of customs duties as a significant revenue source.

d.   Assessment and recommendations on the tax regime

Many aspects of the current tax regime are sound and strong. In particular, the simplicity, stability and moderate tax burden are positive aspects of corporate taxation that must be commended. The importance given to VAT to raise revenue – and the quality of its administration – are strong assets for El Salvador. In addition, the strategic decision to forgo import duties as a revenue-raising mechanism has been wise in the context of El Salvador.

A number of crucial weaknesses and challenges nevertheless remain:

- Some of the incentives provided under the Law on Industrial and Commercial Free Zones and the Law on Export Reactivation are incompatible with the WTO Agreement on Subsidies and Countervailing Measures, as they are directly linked to export performance. In common with about 20 other countries in similar conditions, El Salvador obtained an extension of the transition period to eliminate incompatible incentives by 2015.[46] This was the second extension granted by WTO, and the deadline is unlikely to be pushed again.

- Incentives are designed to attract investments in export-oriented industries or services sectors. With some exceptions, they are not tailored to promoting specific development goals, such as technological upgrading, job creation or cluster development. To a certain extent, the provision of very generous tax incentives on a non-discriminatory basis may be excessive and lead the country to forgo too much revenue.

- The level of tax revenue as a share of GDP is insufficient to allow the Government to provide the extent and quality of public services needed by an aspiring upper middle-income country. To a significant degree, this is the result of the narrow tax basis.

- In spite of the goals stated in the Law on Income Tax, the administrative burden of taxation is excessive and well beyond what could be achieved by adopting international best practices.

- Some widely applied and accepted pro-investment features of corporate taxation are curiously absent in El Salvador, including, in particular, loss carry-forward and accelerated depreciation provisions.

---

[46] Under the WTO Agreement on Subsidies and Countervailing Measures, the least developed countries are exempted from the prohibition of export subsidies. Under certain conditions, countries with a per capita GNP of below $1,000 (at 1990 prices) may be exempted too.

The fiscal reform of 2009 is a welcome indication that the Government is keen to address some of the issues mentioned above – in particular, widening the tax base and avoiding evasion. As indicated above, however, the reform stopped short of introducing structural reforms to the corporate tax regime and to investment incentives. This has been left for a later stage.

Addressing the WTO compliance challenge, however, is a matter of priority and urgency, as the 2015 deadline is approaching fast. It will require a reshaping of investment incentives. It is crucial that El Salvador avail itself of the transition period to formulate and gradually implement a new system of incentives. Abrupt and last-minute changes should be avoided in order to give time to companies that currently enjoy non-compliant incentives to adjust and to contain possible disinvestments. Consultations with investors should also be put in place in a transparent process.

The transition period should be used by El Salvador to implement complementary reforms to address the other challenges highlighted above. The overall goal of the reform would be to preserve an attractive and competitive general tax regime (i.e. available to *all* investors), with limited and targeted incentives to support national development goals. At a time when some of the EPZ incentives and the 6 per cent drawback for exporters need to be phased out, it will be important for El Salvador to resist inevitable calls from the business community to replace these tax breaks with other incentives measures and to multiply sector-specific tax breaks.

The costs and benefits of incentives become more and more complex to assess as they proliferate. It is also increasingly difficult to resist calls for special treatment by one sector when other sectors benefit from specific tax breaks. Ultimately, any sector will be able to make a case that it deserves special treatment for one reason or another. In order to avoid getting onto the slippery slope of a proliferation of incentives, it may, therefore, be worthwhile considering a regime that offers a level playing field to all sectors and investors, with targeted incentives contingent upon general outcomes such as job creation, training or expansion.

In addition, a light administrative burden, stability and transparency should be considered as key ingredients of attractiveness and competitiveness. Ultimately, facilitation services, the ease of doing business, infrastructure, and human resources are the key ingredients in FDI attractiveness and location determinants, even more so than possible corporate income tax holidays. It is interesting to note, in that respect, that tax incentives were listed as only the 8th (out of 10) most relevant factors affecting the decision to invest by foreign investors surveyed for PROESA in 2009.[47] Factors such as proximity to market, economic stability, labour costs and quality of the labour force ranked well ahead of tax incentives. In the case of domestic investors, tax incentives ranked as the least relevant factor.

Concretely, a balanced yet attractive tax regime offering a level playing field to all investors could be achieved through the following measures:

- Unify the tax system by integrating the special regime for corporate taxation created under the Law on Industrial and Commercial Free Zones into a reformed and more attractive general regime (see below). A gradual shift could be established in the transition period to 2015, in order to allow companies operating under this regime to adapt smoothly. This would not only bring El Salvador into compliance with WTO rules, but would also widen the tax basis.

- Carefully review the costs (revenues foregone) and benefits of the incentives provided under the Law on International Services. The option favoured currently by the Ministry of Economy and PROESA appears to be to widen somewhat the applicability of the incentives regime (including in terms of international logistics and distribution, and for medical services). The cost/benefit ratio of

---

[47] Encuesta Clima de Negocios. Septiembre–Noviembre 2009. Herrartemarketing.

the incentives should nevertheless be analysed further. The option of integrating export-oriented services into the reformed general regime should also be looked at, particularly if more targeted incentives are put in place (chapter III).

● Compensate the phasing out of export-dependent incentives with measures to improve the attractiveness of the general regime and actively promote investment. This would help ensure that projects implemented under the EPZ and international services regime are perpetuated, and that new investments are promoted. The measures proposed below would avoid granting complete tax holidays as is currently the case, but would still promote investment and make El Salvador an attractive destination from a tax perspective:

   ✓ Review the level of the headline corporate income tax rate in light of the options considered for the provision of incentives.

   ✓ Allow faster rates of depreciation for tax purposes and introduce accelerated depreciation for certain classes of assets or investments.

   ✓ Introduce a loss carry-forward provision, as a strong pro-investment incentive and to allow companies to benefit from the tax relief provided through faster depreciation.

   ✓ Preserve the extra-territoriality of EPZs and services parks to allow them to import inputs and capital goods free of all duties and VAT.[48]

   ✓ Replace the monthly advance payment requirement on corporate income tax with a quarterly or semi-annual system based on self-assessment.

● Introduce limited and targeted incentives to achieve specific outcomes. These would be linked, in particular, to the promotion of "responsible" and "green" investments that could bring particular benefits to El Salvador in terms of job creation and sustainable investments. Chapter III provides a more complete discussion of these issues – including from the perspective of the EPZs and given the need to re-profile them under WTO-compatible incentives schemes.

● Introduce a new VAT rate to increase revenue while sheltering the poorer segments of the population. Essential goods and services could be taxed below the current 13 per cent (or VAT exemption regime), while non-essential or luxury goods and services, or those generating a negative externality, could be taxed at rate of around 20 per cent.[49]

● Rapidly negotiate and ratify DTTs with the main existing or potential source countries of FDI, in order to avoid double taxation of profits.

2.   International trade agreements

El Salvador's openness policy is reflected in its membership of WTO and in the number of regional or bilateral free trade agreements that it has concluded in recent years. Although it joined the General Agreement on Tariffs and Trade (GATT) only in 1991, El Salvador sought to deepen integration with its neighbours as early as 1960 under the General Treaty on Central American Economic Integration, which

---

[48] Exempting EPZ companies from all indirect taxes is compatible with WTO rules.

[49] Many OECD countries that apply the value-added tax apply differentiated rates according to the nature of the good or service. Some countries in Latin America apply a supplementary sales tax on luxury items. Selected base VAT rates in Latin America are: 21 per cent in Argentina; 19 per cent in Chile; 16 per cent in Colombia; 12 per cent in Guatemala; 15 per cent in Mexico; and 19 per cent in Peru.

created the CACM. A landmark was reached in 2006 with the ratification and entry into force of the CAFTA-DR. The other agreements have typically been negotiated jointly under the CACM framework, and include treaties with Chile, the Dominican Republic, Mexico, Panama, and Taiwan Province of China.

The CACM partners are El Salvador's second-largest export market after the United States, and the most important export market for non-maquila goods. They are also an important potential market for foreign companies that establish operations in El Salvador. Although the objective of establishing a full-fledged customs union has not yet been achieved, the CACM countries have adopted a common external tariff that covers 95 per cent of goods, and most intra-CACM trade is entirely free of duties, subject to rules of origin. The exceptions to the common tariff and duty-free internal trade concern mostly coffee, sugar and oil derivatives. In addition to the liberalization of trade flows, CACM partners have promoted wider objectives of economic integration. The Central American Treaty on Investment and Trade in Services provides the legal framework to encourage the expansion and diversification of trade in services and the promotion and protection of investments.

El Salvador was the first country to ratify CAFTA-DR in March 2006. Although its main purpose is to establish a free trade area, the agreement goes well beyond trade and covers customs administration, government procurement, investment, services, intellectual property rights, labour, the environment, transparency and corruption (see the specific sections in this chapter). The degree of commitments under each of these chapters varies, but is particularly significant in terms of investment, government procurement, services and intellectual property rights.

El Salvador already benefited from preferential access to the United States market before the ratification of CAFTA-DR,[50] and to other Central American countries under the CACM. For its part, El Salvador had reduced its import duties on goods from the United States before 2006. Nevertheless, the agreement solidifies and immediately improved the preferential treatment accorded to Salvadorean goods upon entering the United States. Upon ratification, almost 100 per cent of industrial goods could enter the United States free of import duties, while 89 per cent of agricultural goods could do so. El Salvador, on the other hand, provided duty-free access to 78 per cent and 53 per cent of industrial and agricultural goods from the United States, respectively.

The remaining tariffs will be phased out according to various schedules extending from 5 to 20 years and with linear and non-linear reductions in tariffs. By 2016, all industrial goods from the United States will enter El Salvador free of duties. Protection for agricultural goods will last longer, as 18 per cent of agricultural goods will continue to benefit from some degree of protection between 2016 and 2026. Safeguard measures for agricultural goods are also put in place by all countries, including the United States.

CAFTA-DR does not have a genuine impact on trade among CACM partners, as these countries had already granted each other duty-free access for most goods. The agreement also explicitly stipulates that it does not prevent CACM countries from providing "*identical or more favourable tariff treatment to a good as provided for under the legal instruments of Central American integration*".[51]

An important benefit of CAFTA-DR for El Salvador and other Central American parties lies in the rules of origin applied to determine the eligibility for duty-free access, which are relatively flexible. Inputs from any party to the agreement count as "originating", and thresholds of 35 per cent or 45 per cent are applied when regional value contents criteria must be used.[52] In addition, woven fabrics from Canada and Mexico

---

[50] The United States provided unilateral concessions under the Generalised System of Preferences, the Caribbean Basin Economic Recovery Act, and the United States-Caribbean Basin Trade Partnership Act.

[51] CAFTA-DR, Chapter 3, article 3.3.3.

[52] The threshold is 35 per cent if the method is based on the value of originating materials (build-up method) and 45 per cent if the method is based on the value of non-originating materials (build-down method).

count as originating inputs, and certain fabrics and yarns in insufficient supply within CAFTA-DR parties may be imported from elsewhere and count as originating as well.

El Salvador currently enjoys preferential access to the European Union (EU) market under the Generalized System of Preferences Plus (GSP+). This preferential was under investigation by the European Commission recently because of issues relating to the right to form trade unions and to strike for civil servants. A constitutional amendment solved the issue (section C.6) and the investigation has been terminated.

The labour issue was also a stumbling block in the negotiations for an Association Agreement with the European Union, which would replace the Framework Cooperation Agreement of 1993 as the legal basis for cooperation. The EU policy is to engage in association agreements on a region-to-region basis, rather than with individual countries. The agreement under negotiation intends to give a legal framework to all aspects of the EU's relations with the CACM. It is organized into political dialogue, cooperation, and trade chapters.

Negotiations started in 2007 and are still under way. An eighth round of negotiations was scheduled for July 2009, but was postponed as a result of the situation in Honduras. It is uncertain when negotiations will be completed, even though a recent target was for finalization by 2010. However, it is important for El Salvador to continue to press its CACM partners to reach an agreement with the EU, in order to solidify preferential trade access to the single largest market in the world.

3.   Customs

The efficiency of the customs administration and the extent to which it facilitates trade are essential for the competitiveness of any small, open economy. El Salvador has made significant progress in recent years in improving customs procedures and reducing the time required to export and import goods. Nevertheless, progress remains to be made, and private agents are sending mixed signals about their experiences with customs clearance procedures and delays.

The Central American Uniform Customs Code (CAUCA) and its regulations set a general framework that all CACM countries must adhere to. They define the customs regimes under which goods can be admitted, determine the powers of the customs administration, and set the tariff lines, based on the harmonized system. In addition, member parties of CAFTA-DR have made a number of commitments on customs administration and trade facilitation. Most of these are set in terms of objectives to aim for, but they are nevertheless important. Key among them are commitments in terms of transparency, automation, the use of e-tools, and risk management.

El Salvador does indeed make extensive use of e-tools for customs and risk management. It currently uses UNCTAD's Automated System for Customs Data platform (ASYCUDA++) and is planning to migrate to the latest ASYCUDA World version of the software soon. Under the ASYCUDA platform, El Salvador has applied a selective risk management system based on three channels of clearance.

Improvements in customs administration are reflected in the rate of physical inspections, which fell from 24 per cent of shipments in 2006 to 7.5 per cent in the first four months of 2009. The customs administration also put in place the PACE (Programa Aduanero de Cumplimiento Empresarial) programme in order to pre-certify some importers with the customs administration and facilitate their operations. As of mid-2009, 75 importers had been invited to participate in the programme. Eleven of these had been authorized, and six were rejected for not complying with the necessary criteria.[53]

---

[53] The remaining ones either did not wish to apply to the programme, or cases are pending.

In addition to these efforts, the customs administration established a physical one-stop window for importers in 2007, as part of the El Salvador Eficiente programme. As a result, the World Bank's *Doing Business* indicators show that the times for exporting and importing have been reduced to 14 and 10 days respectively in 2009, down from 22 and 30 days in 2007. In addition, the customs administration reports that the cost to importers has been reduced too.

In spite of these efforts and achievements, progress remains to be made, and the customs administration ought to focus even more on trade facilitation and less on revenue collection. The Directorate-General of Customs recently established its vision, mission and objectives. The vision is defined as being a "model [institution] at the Latin American level (…) to achieve the balance between trade facilitation and control."[54] Its stated objectives include: (a) eliminating tax evasion and generating revenue; (b) fighting against smuggling; (c) cutting clearance times; and (d) improving customs procedures.

Given its open-economy development model, it is suggested that the Government put even greater emphasis on improving the customs administration and mobilize the necessary resources to do so. Concretely, this implies that:

- El Salvador should benchmark its trade facilitation services against the world's most efficient and diligent customs administrations, e.g. Denmark, Hong Kong (China) or Singapore. El Salvador ought to compare itself globally and look beyond Latin America. The exercise could be conducted with technical assistance from the World Customs Organization (WCO), or using the WCO's Customs International Benchmarking Manual.

- El Salvador would benefit from further increasing the use of e-tools in customs administration. The physical one-stop window should be turned into a virtual one where all services are accessible via the internet. WCO guidelines and technical assistance would prove valuable in that respect as well.

- The migration from ASYCUDA++ to ASYCUDA World should be seen as a high priority, as the new platform allows the full use of internet-based e-governance tools. Such tools would also help El Salvador to implement the WCO SAFE Framework of Standards to Secure and Facilitate Global Trade, to which the country has adhered, and to put into place the virtual one-stop window.

- In order to fully reflect the importance given to trade facilitation as opposed to revenue collection and to entrench the mentality change, it would be useful to adjust the vision, mission and objectives statements of the customs administration. The vision should be to become a model of efficiency and diligence at the global level, not just at the Latin American level. Objectives of trade facilitation and efficiency should be reflected more prominently vis-à-vis objectives of revenue collection and the fight against smuggling.

4. Foreign exchange arrangements

The United States dollar was adopted as legal tender on 1 January 2001, with the adoption of the Law on Monetary Integration.[55] Although the Salvadorean colón retains permanent legal tender status, all prices, contracts and non-cash payments are denominated in dollars. There remain few colones in circulation, as banks are required to convert colón notes and coins into dollars.

The stated purpose of the dollarization was to integrate El Salvador into the world economy by facilitating trade and financial flows. It was also intended that it would promote economic stability and

---

[54] Dirección General de Aduanas de El Salvador, Guía Aduanera, primera edición 2008.
[55] Ley de Integración Monetaria.

investment, including through lower interest rates. This has indeed been the case, even though El Salvador is now exposed to fluctuations of the dollar vis-à-vis other major currencies that it cannot influence.

5.   Competition regulations

El Salvador's first Law on Competition[56] came into force on 1 January 2006 together with the establishment of the independent competition regulator, the Superintendence of Competition. Prior to that, the country had limited regulations on competition contained in the Law on Consumer Protection.[57] In a very short period of time, El Salvador has put in place a modern and comprehensive regulatory framework and started to implement it effectively through a competent and proactive competition authority.

The authorities built on the experiences of Brazil, the European Union and Mexico, among others, in drafting the Law on Competition and its implementation decree. The outcome is a high-quality regulatory framework. Importantly, the law applies on a near-universal basis, covering all sectors (including sectors subject to the regulatory oversight of other public bodies) and entities (private as well as public). The only exceptions are the activities reserved by the Constitution to the State or municipalities.

The law addresses four main competition issues: (a) anti-competitive agreements; (b) unfair competitive practices; (c) abuse of dominant position; and (d) economic concentration. A number of specific anti-competitive behaviours and unfair practices are defined and prohibited in the law, including horizontal and vertical agreements. Similarly, the law provides adequate definitions of a dominant position and what constitutes abuses. More specific and detailed regulations are set in the implementation decree to define the methodologies to be used by the Superintendence of Competition, including on relevant market and relevant product. In the case of economic concentration, the law sets a threshold below which prior authorization is not required,[58] and it also allows certain concentrations to take place if they bring efficiency or other benefits to the economy.

The law establishes the Superintendence of Competition as a strong and independent regulatory body, and the Government rightfully invested significant financial and human resources to turn it into an efficient organization quickly. Rulings on competition cases are the competence of the Board, which includes the superintendent, two directors and three substitutes. All members of the Board are appointed for five-year terms, but only the superintendent's position is full-time. Only the superintendent and the two directors are allowed to vote, but the three substitutes are expected to attend sessions and have the right to express opinions.

The Board has relatively wide powers, which include: (a) imposing precautionary measures; (b) imposing fines of up to 5,000 times the monthly minimum urban wage in the relevant industry;[59] and (c) ordering remedial obligations to stop uncompetitive practices and/or imposing changes of behaviour or structure. Board rulings can be appealed to the administrative chamber of the Supreme Court, like all decisions of administrative bodies.

In just over three years since its creation, the Superintendence has firmly established itself in El Salvador's institutional landscape and built a strong track record of operational work. Coordination and cooperation agreements have already been signed with 11 public institutions, including the sectoral regulators in electricity, telecommunications and finance, and the customs administration. These are very positive steps in ensuring that competition regulations are applied across all sectors of the economy.

---

[56] Ley de Competencia.

[57] Ley de Protección al Consumidor.

[58] The threshold is equivalent to 50,000 times the annual urban minimum wage in the relevant industry. This amounts to around $110 million.

[59] Higher fines may be imposed in particularly serious cases. Fines can reach 6 per cent of annual sales, 6 per cent of assets, or 2 to 10 times the estimated gain derived from the uncompetitive practices.

The Superintendence has also carried out or commissioned around 20 sectoral studies in the past three years, and more are planned for the years to come.[60] The studies, together with the cases brought to its attention, have led the Superintendence to make policy recommendations on competition issues to various ministries and public administrations. A relatively large number of competition cases and filings for mergers and acquisitions have also been investigated by the Superintendence, either on its own initiative or following a formal complaint by an interested party. While many of the competition cases have been dismissed early on, the Superintendence has imposed fines and remedial actions in 12 cases.

Efforts to enforce competition regulations have been frustrated, however, by the lengthy appeals procedure. Of the 12 cases on which a ruling was issued, all but one have been appealed. No appeal procedure has reached a conclusion yet, and the Supreme Court has not developed sufficient competence to rule on competition cases.

In the three years since it first adopted a competition law, El Salvador has made impressive yet incomplete progress towards using the regulatory framework to improve the overall competitiveness and efficiency of the economy and promote consumers' interests. El Salvador voluntarily subjected itself to a Peer Review of Competition Law and Policy led by the Organization for Economic Cooperation and Development (OECD) in 2008. The review concluded that "in less than three years El Salvador is off to a good – one might say excellent – start. Its experience can serve, in some ways at least, as an example of an effective way to begin to implement a competition policy".[61]

The key weakness in the framework lies not in competition regulations, but in the wider issue of the efficiency and speed of the judicial system. The slow appeals procedure encourages companies to contest the rulings of the Board. In addition, until the administrative chamber of the Supreme Court rules on a few cases, there will be a great deal of uncertainty regarding its interpretation of the Law on Competition. The Attorney-General should thus make all possible and legitimate efforts to speed the resolution of cases currently subject to an appeals procedure.

In turn, it is essential that the judges sitting in the administrative chamber of the Supreme Court receive adequate training on competition issues, not only on the purely legal aspects, but also on the economic aspects. Although much of this training might have to be conducted autonomously by the judges to respect their independence, the Superintendence might be in a position to prepare advanced training material not specifically aimed at judges, but which judges could use. Local universities and international organizations might also be in a position to contribute to training without compromising the judges' independence.

A second area where significant improvements could be achieved is in terms of advocacy of competition policy in Government. The Superintendence has already made significant efforts in this respect, by preparing and publishing policy recommendations for ministries and public administrations. Such advice is non-binding, however. In order to ensure that a competition perspective is appropriately reflected across all key Government policies, it would be useful for the Cabinet to adopt a formal competition policy. Adopted by consensus, the policy would provide a framework for sectoral policies to comply with. This would be particularly important for policies on infrastructure concessions and agriculture, and would foster the economy's overall competitiveness.

6. Labour regulations

Basic labour rights and standards are granted a high level of importance, as they are subject to constitutional treatment. Besides guaranteeing general principles such as non-discrimination in wages, the right to sign collective agreements, the right to form trade unions and employers' associations, and the

---

[60] Some of these studies were conducted with technical assistance from UNCTAD under the COMPAL (Competition and Consumer Protection Policies for Latin America) project.
[61] OECD (2008), page 7.

right to strike, the Constitution also fixes the normal working day at eight hours and the standard working week at 44 hours, the minimum employment age, and the requirement to establish by law a minimum wage sufficient to ensure basic needs. The Constitution also mandates that employees and employers contribute to the social security fund and that a workers' training system be established.

The Labour Code[62] provides a detailed but flexible set of labour rules. El Salvador ranks eighty-seventh in the World Bank's *Doing Business* indicator on "employing workers", but is still behind Costa Rica and Nicaragua. Employers and foreign investors generally commend the labour force for being hard-working, productive, committed and relatively trainable. In addition, employer–union relations are good and El Salvador is not affected by significant disputes or strikes. Employers nevertheless raise concerns about the level and quality of training of graduates, the lack of English or poor knowledge of English, and the insufficient depth of the trained workforce.

The Labour Code strikes an adequate balance between protecting workers' rights and providing flexibility to employers in hiring and firing so as to promote job creation. The Code applies equally in export processing zones and in the rest of the economy. Three types of contracts are allowed: (a) indefinite-term; (b) fixed-term; and (c) seasonal. The law does not set a maximum duration for fixed-term contracts, but it stipulates that contracts that relate to permanent tasks in an enterprise are considered indefinite, regardless of the actual terms of the contract. This provides additional protection and certainty to workers, and it does not put excessive stress on employers as there is sufficient flexibility in the Code to terminate indefinite contracts. The Code also allows a relatively short trial period of 30 days.

The procedures for firings and for the termination of contracts are relatively flexible. Four broad categories are defined by law:

- Termination without responsibility for either party (with or without judicial intervention) includes closing or downsizing (subject to conditions) the company, or the incapacity of one of the parties. It is not subject to any compensation.

- Worker-related grounds for termination without compensation are precisely defined in the law. Behaviours that may justify termination include repeated negligence, violation of company secrets, or unjustifiably failing to report to work for two consecutive days or three days in a month.

- A number of circumstances are defined that allow a worker to consider the contract terminated and still to benefit from compensations as provided for in cases of redundancies. These include unjustified wage cuts and mistreatment or dangerous working conditions.

- Termination of contract by mutual agreement does not generate any obligation on either party.

All firings that do not fall within the reasons justified by law are considered without cause. In such cases, the employer is required to pay the equivalent of 30 days of wages (excluding other benefits) per year of employment. The wage used to calculate the compensation is capped at four times the minimum wage, however.

Minimum wages are set and reviewed at least every three years by the National Council on Minimum Wages, which includes three representatives from the Government, two from trade unions and two from employers' associations. Eight different levels of minimum wages are set, depending on the sector of activity, ranging from $2.7 per day in cotton picking to $5.79 per day in maquilas and $6.92 per day in retail and services.[63]

---

[62] Código de Trabajo.

[63] The eight sectors are: (a) agriculture; (b) coffee picking; (c) sugar cane picking; (d) cotton picking; (e) seasonal agricultural workers; (f) commerce and services; (g) industry; and (h) maquilas.

In addition to salaries, employers are mandated to contribute 7.5 per cent and 6.75 per cent of wages to the social security and private pension funds, respectively. Employers with more than 10 workers are also required to contribute 1 per cent of wages to the Instituto Salvadoreño de Formación Profesional (INSAFORP). INSAFORP is an autonomous public agency in charge of promoting continuous learning in the labour force. It does not provide training itself, but provides partial funding to companies offering internal or external training to their workers, usually with a cap of, at most, twice the company's initial contribution to the fund, through the 1 per cent levy.

The degree of unionization is relatively low in El Salvador, as is the incidence of strikes. Workers' rights are nevertheless adequately protected, even though strikes are subject to a number of conditions, including a secret voting procedure and prior notification. Lockouts are subject to prior notification and are authorized only to defend the economic interests of the employer. Until mid-2009, the Constitution forbade workers in the public sector and municipalities from striking, and the right to form trade unions was denied to civil servants. Articles 47–48 of the Constitution were amended in May 2009 in order to allow civil servants to defend their interests through trade unions.[64] They were also granted the right to strike, except for those working in essential public services.

Reforms to the Labour Code are not called for at the moment, as it provides an adequate balance between protecting workers and providing the flexibility needed to promote job creation. It is particularly noteworthy that the Constitution was amended in order to bring the country into conformity with ILO Convention 87 and solve the issue of the rights of civil servants. El Salvador had been under investigation by the European Commission since 2008 on this issue, which posed a threat regarding the preferential trade access to the EU market. Following the amendments to the Constitution, the European Commission terminated the investigation October 2009.

7.   Employment of foreigners and access to skills

The employment of foreign workers is regulated by the Labour Code and the Law on Migration.[65] The approach adopted regarding access to foreign skills and workers in these laws is antiquated, and does not reflect recent practices that have been successfully implemented in a number of countries that have proactively used immigration as a development tool. The Law on Migration dates back to 1958, and has not been amended since minor revisions were adopted in the 1960s.

The experience of numerous countries shows that allowing the temporary – and under certain conditions, permanent – entry of expatriate workers can be a very useful way to fill skills gaps in the economy, promote transfers of skills and know-how, and generate a cross-fertilization of competences and work practices. Even economies that have with the most advanced education systems in the world allow the temporary or permanent entry of foreign workers in a systematic way to fill certain skills gaps. Some, such as Australia, Canada, Dubai and Singapore, go as far as proactively attracting skilled expatriates as a development tool.

A revision to the Law on Migration is currently under preparation. The process was at an early stage during the UNCTAD fact-finding mission in May 2009, and a draft law was not available for discussion. Consequently, the discussion below is based on the current law. However, indications are that the revision to the law as currently envisaged would not lead to a fundamental shift in the regulatory approach on the entry of foreign workers.

The Labour Code stipulates that Salvadorean nationals must account for at least 90 per cent of the labour force of any company, and 85 per cent of wages. As a reflection of historical factors and the regional

---

[64] Limitations remain for certain classes of public workers, including members of the armed forces, the police, and high-ranking decision-makers.
[65] Ley de Migración.

integration process, however, nationals from Central American countries (Costa Rica, Guatemala, Honduras and Nicaragua) count as Salvadoreans for the calculation of these requirements. In addition, up to four management positions can be filled by foreigners without counting in the calculation of the thresholds.

The Ministry of Labour and the Directorate-General of Migration indicate that they have adopted a flexible attitude towards issuing work permits for expatriates, which they report are granted as long as companies comply with the 90 per cent and 85 per cent requirements. The Law on Migration nevertheless stipulates that permits should be granted on condition that the migrant workers fill a gap and do not substitute for Salvadoreans that have similar skills. Yet, no precise labour market testing procedure is defined.

Work permits are issued for a maximum period of one year and are linked to the employer. They may be renewed up to four times, but no foreign worker is allowed to be employed in El Salvador for more than five years, except in exceptional circumstances. El Salvador also requires that a bond equivalent to the cost of a return plane ticket be deposited upon issuance of the work permit.

A second avenue is available for foreigners to work or run businesses in El Salvador, as the country may issue a permanent residence card with working rights and without prior temporary residence requirements. A number of conditions apply, however, including not replacing or competing with Salvadoreans. Given these conditions, this option has not been used extensively. It must be noted also that nationals by birth of Costa Rica, Guatemala, Honduras, Nicaragua and Panama are able to work in El Salvador easily. They may indeed acquire permanent residence status, together with working rights, upon simple request, once they have entered El Salvador legally.

In 2008, El Salvador issued fewer than 1,400 work permits for foreigners (excluding Central American nationals). The countries with the highest representation are China, Colombia, Mexico, the Republic of Korea, and the United States. This figure is extremely low, as it represents the total number of foreigners (excluding Central American nationals) working legally in the country.[66] As a comparison, the United States set a quota of up to 85,000 HI-B visas for specialized foreign workers in 2010. These visas have a maximum duration of three years, and one can thus estimate that around 250,000 foreigners may be working in the United States under HI-B status alone. In addition, the country allocates around 50,000 permanent residency cards per year through a lottery system, and there are other types of work permits for foreigners.

The relative number of specialized and skilled foreign workers with temporary residence is thus significantly higher in the United States than in El Salvador.[67] Much more strikingly, Singapore – which has based much of its development on foreign skills – had an expatriate labour force on temporary residence permits of 1 million people in 2008, out of a total labour force of 2.9 million.

This obviously does not mean that El Salvador should seek to increase the presence of expatriates as a goal per se. Nevertheless, the country would benefit from implementing a modern and user-friendly approach to granting work permits for expatriates. This would help El Salvador fill temporary skills shortages while the long-term education and training policy yields concrete results, and it could, of itself, contribute to transfers of skills and know-how. It would also promote an increase in FDI flows, and would be particularly important as El Salvador seeks to attract more technologically advanced investments.

The need for skilled expatriates may be more important in the near and medium term, as skills shortages remain significant. However, El Salvador should not consider that it will no longer benefit from foreign workers after it has built a stronger education system, as illustrated by the situation and policies of high-income countries. A new system of allocating work permits is thus recommended, which would protect

---

[66] Given that work permits have a maximum duration of one year, the number of permits issued in a given year is equivalent to the number of legal expatriate workers.

[67] With a population of 312 million people, the 250,000 HI-B visas in the United States represent 0.08 per cent of the total. With a population of 6.2 million people, 1,371 work permits for non–Central Americans represent 0.02 per cent of the total.

the interests of the national labour force while ensuring the availability of qualified workers and promoting skills transfers.

The new system would be centred on one main type of work permit for foreigners, with the following characteristics:

- **Temporary:** The permit would be temporary and issued for up to three years at a time, instead of the current one-year limit. It would be renewable once, for another three years, and would combine the work and residence permit. Although the nature of the work permit is temporary, El Salvador should allow workers to apply for permanent residence after six years, subject to certain conditions such as possessing particularly valuable skills.

- **Skill-based:** The permit would be issued for workers who possess certain skills that are in short supply among nationals. The United States issues H1-B visas for "specialty occupations"[68] and requires the completion of a bachelor's degree. It would be useful for El Salvador to define eligible skills relatively broadly and not to demand a university degree, as many potentially valuable skills are acquired through other channels. Rather than defining a precise list of occupations eligible for the permit, El Salvador could define broad categories of occupations for which employers are allowed to recruit foreigners. These broad categories (e.g. engineers, computer scientists or teachers) would be defined after consultations with all relevant stakeholders, including employers' federations, trade unions and civil society. They would be based on an audit of national skills and labour market needs[69] and would be reviewed periodically.

- **Subject to national quota:** A quota would be set annually, based on the same consultations with stakeholders. It would apply nationally and to all occupations. Under such a system, it would no longer be necessary to apply the current 10 and 15 per cent rules on employees and wages at the company level, as the interests of the Salvadorean labour force would be protected by the quota at the national level. As they stand, the 10 and 15 per cent rules tend not be binding, in any case. In addition, a national quota would tend to offer more flexibility at the company level.

- **Within profession:** The permit would allow foreigners to work within the profession for which they have been trained, not in any other occupation.

- **Employer-based:** The permit would be issued upon request from an employer, meaning that a foreigner would be eligible for entry only after having secured a job offer from a bona fide company established in El Salvador.

- **No labour-market testing:** Employers would not have to justify not having been able to identify a suitable Salvadorean before applying for a work permit for an expatriate, as long as the visa is issued within the national quota.

- **Credential checks and profiling:** Issuance of a work permit and entry into El Salvador would be conditional upon verification of the candidate's qualifications and usual profiling.

- **Wages:** In order to prevent the use of foreign skilled workers at a lower cost, employers would be required to pay at least the prevailing wage for the applicable occupation and level of responsibility.

---

[68] Speciality occupations are defined as those that require the theoretical and practical application of a body of highly specialized knowledge. The United States does not establish precise lists of eligible occupations, however.

[69] INSAFORP would be well placed to make a contribution in this respect.

- **Spouse's benefits:** It would be useful for El Salvador to grant a work permit to the spouses of eligible workers. This is likely to be a condition for many of the most skilled workers to accept a job in El Salvador. In addition, the spouses of skilled people tend to be skilled themselves, which puts them in a position to make a contribution to the economy.

In addition to this work permit programme, it would be useful to allow companies, under more stringent conditions, to recruit skilled foreign workers either beyond the national quota set above, or outside of the pre-defined occupation categories. Recruitment of expatriates under these circumstances would require a labour market test to demonstrate that no Salvadorean could be found to fill the position. The work permit would also be issued for a renewable period of three years.

8. Land

Ownership of agricultural land is a historically sensitive issue and remains subject to surface limitations for both nationals and foreigners. By contrast, ownership of non-agricultural land and land for industrial purposes in rural areas is unrestricted and subject to the same regulations for foreigners and nationals. In addition, El Salvador has made great progress over the past decade in implementing an efficient and comprehensive registry of titles and cadastre.

Until the land reforms of the 1980s, ownership was highly concentrated among a small number of families, while the majority of peasants grew subsistence crops on lower-quality land. The reforms expropriated large landowners and redistributed agricultural land to cooperatives and individuals. Under article 105 of the Constitution, ownership of agricultural land by a single natural or legal person is currently limited to a maximum of 245 hectares.[70] In addition, article 109 stipulates that foreigners are allowed to own agricultural land only if Salvadoreans are granted reciprocal rights in the former's country of origin.[71]

As noted above, foreigners have access to ownership of non-agricultural land without discrimination. Fully serviced plots are readily available in export processing zones and industrial zones. Export processing zones, in turn, are owned and run mostly by the private sector, including foreigners.

El Salvador has reformed its cadastre and land registry system to provide secure property titles, facilitate transactions and promote investment in land. The cadastre and land registry are both fully computerized and recently received the ISO:9001 certification. As part of the efforts to facilitate administrative processes, the National Geographic and Cadastre Institute[72] and the Registry of Real Estate and Mortgages[73] were integrated in the National Registry Centre, together with the registry of commerce and registry of intellectual property. This good performance is illustrated by El Salvador's forty-sixth place in the "registering property" category of the World Bank's *Doing Business* indicators for 2010.

Access to land for industrial purposes and the safety of land titles is thus not a problem for investors. The surface limitation, however, is a potential barrier to FDI in agriculture. As highlighted in UNCTAD's *World Investment Report 2009: Transnational Corporations, Agricultural Production and Development*,[74] foreign investors' involvement in crop production can take several forms. The traditional form used to be direct ownership of plantations. Under such an arrangement, TNCs need to be allowed to own large areas of land, as most are interested only in large-scale production.[75]

---

[70] The limitation does not apply to farmers' cooperatives.
[71] The reciprocity condition does not apply for land in rural areas that is destined for industrial use.
[72] Instituto Geográfico y del Catastro Nacional.
[73] Registro de la Propiedad Raíz e Hipotecas.
[74] UNCTAD (2009h).
[75] With the possible exception of niche or smaller-sized investors, e.g. in floriculture, which requires smaller surfaces.

Increasingly, however, large food TNCs such as Chiquita, Del Monte, Dole, Nestlé, SAB Miller and Sime Darby have relied on contract farming. Although there are various forms of contract farming (chapter III, section C.3), the most common type involves a TNC buying produce from a large number of (often small-scale) farmers, to whom it provides various extension services (seeds, fertilizers, technical support, quality controls, financing). Under contract farming arrangements, TNCs do not necessarily need to be allowed to own any agricultural land. Their involvement in a country, however, can be beneficial, as it can help small-scale farmers to move out of subsistence agriculture and adopt modern farming techniques.

The legal restrictions on agricultural land ownership are not a barrier to TNC involvement in agricultural production through contract farming. They are a major impediment, however, to direct TNC participation in the production of cash crops. If El Salvador wishes to attract significant foreign equity participation in the sector, it would need to consider lifting the 245-hectare limitation, at least on a selective basis. If this were not socially and politically desirable, El Salvador may still wish to attract TNC participation in agriculture through contract farming in order to promote the modernization of the sector and raise rural incomes (chapter III).

9. Environmental regulations

Environmental regulations are particularly important to El Salvador, as the country is very vulnerable to environmental degradation. The high population density,[76] the mountainous topography and erodible soils, past deforestation and relatively low levels of availability of fresh water per capita all contribute to this vulnerability. In spite of this, El Salvador only recently adopted a specific legal framework on the environment.

The first Law on Environment[77] was adopted in 1998, and it complements other legal instruments related to the environment.[78] It led to the establishment of various institutions in charge of managing environmental issues, centred on the Ministry of Environment and Natural Resources (Ministerio de Medio Ambiente y Recursos Naturales ((MARN) and the National System of Management of the Environment (Sistema Nacional de Gestión del Medio Ambiente (SINAMA)). The SINAMA is coordinated by the MARN, and includes representatives of various ministries, autonomous agencies and municipalities with competencies related to the environment. It is in charge of coordinating sectoral and intersectoral activities to achieve the objectives of the law in terms of environmental management, and to help the MARN prepare the biannual report on the state of the environment. In addition to the law, El Salvador adopted an environmental policy in 2000 that was complemented by the environmental chapter of the government strategy *País Seguro 2004–2009* and the national environmental strategy of 2004.

The Law on Environment provides a generally sound legal framework for the protection of the environment. It firmly establishes the objective of achieving environmentally sustainable development and the principles of prevention and precaution. It creates a number of mechanisms to protect the environment, but it relies heavily on environmental permitting and environmental impact assessments (EIAs). Most investments must file a project description to the MARN using the environmental form (formulario ambiental). The MARN then determines whether an EIA is needed prior to issuance of the environmental permit. The terms of reference of the EIA are determined on a case-by-case basis by the MARN.

EIAs are required by law for 15 broadly defined categories of investments, in addition to "any other project that may have considerable and irreversible impacts on the environment, human health and well-being or the ecosystem".[79] The consequence of this provision is that it is difficult for investors to know *ex ante* whether their project requires an EIA or not.

---

[76] At close to 340 inhabitants per square kilometre, El Salvador has by far the highest population density in non-insular Latin America.
[77] Ley del Medio Ambiente.
[78] These include the Law on Forestry, Law on Protected Natural Areas, Law on the Control of Pesticides, and Law on Mining, among others.
[79] Law on Environment, article 21.

In late 2006, there was a backlog of about 2,500 EIAs to be reviewed, and the environmental permitting procedure had become a serious bottleneck to investment.[80] The MARN subsequently succeeded in clearing much of the backlog, including by increasing its technical capacity. The implementation decree to the Law on Environment was also amended in order to define three categories of projects for environmental permitting purposes:

- Projects with no or low environmental consequences need not file any documentation to the Ministry;

- Projects with light, moderate or high environmental consequences must file preliminary documentation (formulario ambiental), and are separated into two categories after initial evaluation by the Ministry:

  ✓ Projects with light impact do not require full EIAs but must obtain the environmental permit.

  ✓ Projects with moderate or high impact require full EIAs, based on the terms of references as defined by the Ministry.

This amendment was accompanied by the publication of a detailed categorization of projects according to the three groups above, which clarifies the requirements for investors. The MARN indicated that there is currently no backlog of projects pending review and that it is able to assess EIAs within the 60-day period mandated by law. The nature and extent of the EIAs, however, continue to be determined on a case-by-case basis by the Ministry, as per the terms of reference.

Aside from EIAs, the Law on Environment establishes a number of other mechanisms to promote environmental sustainability, including the national environmental strategy and policy, the environmental strategy evaluations (ESEs), public consultations on EIAs, and environmental education. As mentioned above, however, the emphasis so far has been on EIAs. In particular, the ESE mechanism − through which the consistency with the national environmental strategy and the environmental impact of all government policies and programmes are to be evaluated and minimized − has not been put to full use.

A number of measures could thus be adopted to further improve environmental regulations and promote sustainable development:

- **Prepare a policy and strategy for environmentally sustainable development:** As a country with a relatively fragile environment, El Salvador would benefit from preparing a policy and strategy for environmentally sustainable development. Such a policy would underpin government policies, programmes and plans in a wide range of areas, including industry, infrastructure development (energy choices, modes of transport), agriculture, tourism, urban planning and others. Although this is partly done under the environmental policy, a more comprehensive approach aimed towards sustainable growth and development would be more effective.

- **Strengthen the ESE mechanism:** The environmentally sustainable development policy should be an opportunity to revitalize the ESE mechanism. Integrating consideration for environmental sustainability into all relevant government programmes would require a strong institutional mechanism, which could be led by the SINAMA. Such a mechanism has been successfully adopted in a rising number of countries, including in Latin America, and El Salvador could draw lessons from these experiences. This would also help El Salvador determine environmental impact mitigation requirements at the sectoral level, instead of at the project level as is currently the case through

---

[80] World Bank (2007).

the environmental permitting process. It would also speed up the procedures for investors and prevent new backlogs from arising on EIA assessments.

- **Complete the set of technical norms and regulations**: El Salvador still lacks a number of technical norms and regulations, including in terms of air and water pollution. This gap ought to be filled, building on international standards. Preparing standard terms of references for EIAs for certain types of projects would also be a practical way to ease the requirements imposed upon investors without compromising environmental protection.

10. Intellectual property law

Substantial revisions to the intellectual property framework were passed in 2005 and 2006 in order to comply with the commitments made under CAFTA-DR. The intellectual property rights chapter of CAFTA-DR is quite comprehensive, and raises the standard of protection above the requirements of the WTO agreement on Trade-related Aspects of Intellectual Property Rights (TRIPS). In addition, CAFTA-DR requires parties to ratify a number of international agreements.[81]

CAFTA-DR covers trademarks, geographical indications, domain names on the internet, patents, copyrights and related rights, and encrypted program-carrying satellite signals. It also entails general and specific obligations in terms of enforcement. These obligations have been translated into national law under the Law on Intellectual Property and the Law on Trademarks and Other Distinctive Signs.[82] The main provisions of these laws are as follows:

- Copyright and related rights protect authors, performers and producers of a broad range of literary, artistic and scientific works. Moral rights are protected for an indefinite term, and the protection of economic rights was increased from 50 to 70 years. The law establishes detailed provisions on contracts to transfer economic rights.

- Patent protection over products and processes is available for 20 years. At the request of the right-holder, the terms of a patent may be adjusted to last longer to compensate for unreasonable delays in the process of granting the patent.

- Trademark registration is valid for 10 years, renewable indefinitely for successive 10-year periods. Well-known trademarks and distinctive signs are protected in accordance with the Paris Convention. Geographical indications may be registered as trademarks, as long as they are not used in the course of trade in relation to a product or service where that indication is false or misleading with respect to the geographical origin of the product or service.

- Trade names, emblems, expressions or signs of commercial advertising, certification marks, and appellations of origin may be registered for an indefinite duration.

- Plant varieties may be protected through patents. El Salvador is committed under CAFTA-DR to ratify the International Convention for the Protection of New Varieties of Plants (UPOV Convention), but it has not done so yet.

Compulsory licences may be granted by a competent court in case of declared emergency or national security situation and to satisfy the basic needs of the local population. Such licences are non-exclusive and may not be assigned to others. The judicial declaration granting them must include the following minimum requirements: (a) scope and duration (limited to the purpose for which it was authorized); (b) amount and

---

[81] Including the WIPO Copyright Treaty, the Patent Cooperation Treaty, the Trademark Law Treaty and the International Convention for the Protection of New Varieties of Plants.

[82] Ley de Propiedad Intelectual and Ley de Marcas y Otros Signos Distinctivos.

form of payment of remuneration for the right-holder; (c) conditions necessary to fulfil its purpose; and (d) to supply the internal market.

Intellectual property rights are protected through administrative, civil and criminal proceedings. El Salvador has set up a specialized intellectual property unit in the Office of the Attorney-General and has created special intellectual property courts. The two laws have detailed rules to implement preliminary or permanent injunctions, initiate civil actions and determine amounts of damages. The Criminal Code sanctions infringement of intellectual property rights with up to six years in jail.

Law enforcement agencies have the authority to seize suspected pirated and counterfeit goods in the country or at the border, and also the equipment used to make or transmit them and any documentary evidence. Courts have the authority to order the destruction of counterfeit goods, unless the right-holder consents to an alternate disposition.

The Ministry of Economy has endeavoured to coordinate all relevant institutions, including the police force, the customs administration, the judicial authorities, the intellectual property register and the Attorney-General in the "Comité Interinstitucional de Observancia de la Propiedad Intelectual" to improve the enforcement of intellectual property rights. As a result of its regulatory and enforcement policies, El Salvador has put in place a protective framework for intellectual property rights. Unlike other CAFTA-DR members, the United States authorities have never listed El Salvador as a country of significant concern for intellectual property rights infringements.

11. Selected sectoral regulations

a. Electricity and telecommunications

El Salvador engaged early on in liberalization of the electricity and telecommunication sectors, following closely on the footsteps of pioneering countries in the region and beyond. It was in the first wave of developing countries to adjust their regulatory framework with the purpose of creating a competitive framework in industries that had long been considered as natural state monopolies or strategic sectors that needed to remain under government control.[83] As technology progressed (e.g. with the development of the internet and mobile telephony) and the regulatory approach to electricity and telecommunications evolved around the world, El Salvador made the strategic choice to introduce competition where feasible, to allow the entry of FDI, and to privatize a large proportion of public assets (chapter I).

The General Superintendence for Electricity and Telecommunications (Superintendencia General de Electricidad y Telecomunicaciones (SIGET)) was established in 1997 as an independent regulatory agency for both electricity and telecommunications, at the same time as the General Law on Electricity[84] and the Law on Telecommunications[85] were adopted. El Salvador vested strong powers in SIGET, and granted it administrative as well as financial autonomy in order to establish the credibility of the new regulatory framework. In a relatively short time span, SIGET has succeeded in establishing a good track record as a strong and competent agency. As mandated by law, it has also established a good working relationship with the Superintendence of Competition. The two agencies have signed a memorandum of understanding and exchanged staff. In addition, the Superintendence completed a competition review of the electricity sector in 2007, which provided a number of recommendations, including in terms of requirements to purchase power under long-term contracts and the load dispatch rule on the spot market.

---

[83] This was particularly the case for electricity, but also true of telecommunications.

[84] Ley General de Electricidad.

[85] Ley de Telecomunicaciones.

El Salvador built on the Chilean experience in drafting the General Law on Electricity. The law states among its core objectives the establishment of a competitive market, free access for generators to the transmission and distribution lines, the rational use of resources, and development of the infrastructure. Figure II.2 illustrates the structure of the electricity market.

Figure II.2. Structure of the electricity market

MRS (spot market supply) → ← Long-term contracts

Transmission (monopoly)

UT (load dispatch centre)

Cross-ownerships allowed

Generator a | Generator b | Generator c | Generator d

Distributor a | Distributor b | Distributor c | Distributor d

Retailer a | Retailer b | Retailer c | Retailer d

FINAL USERS

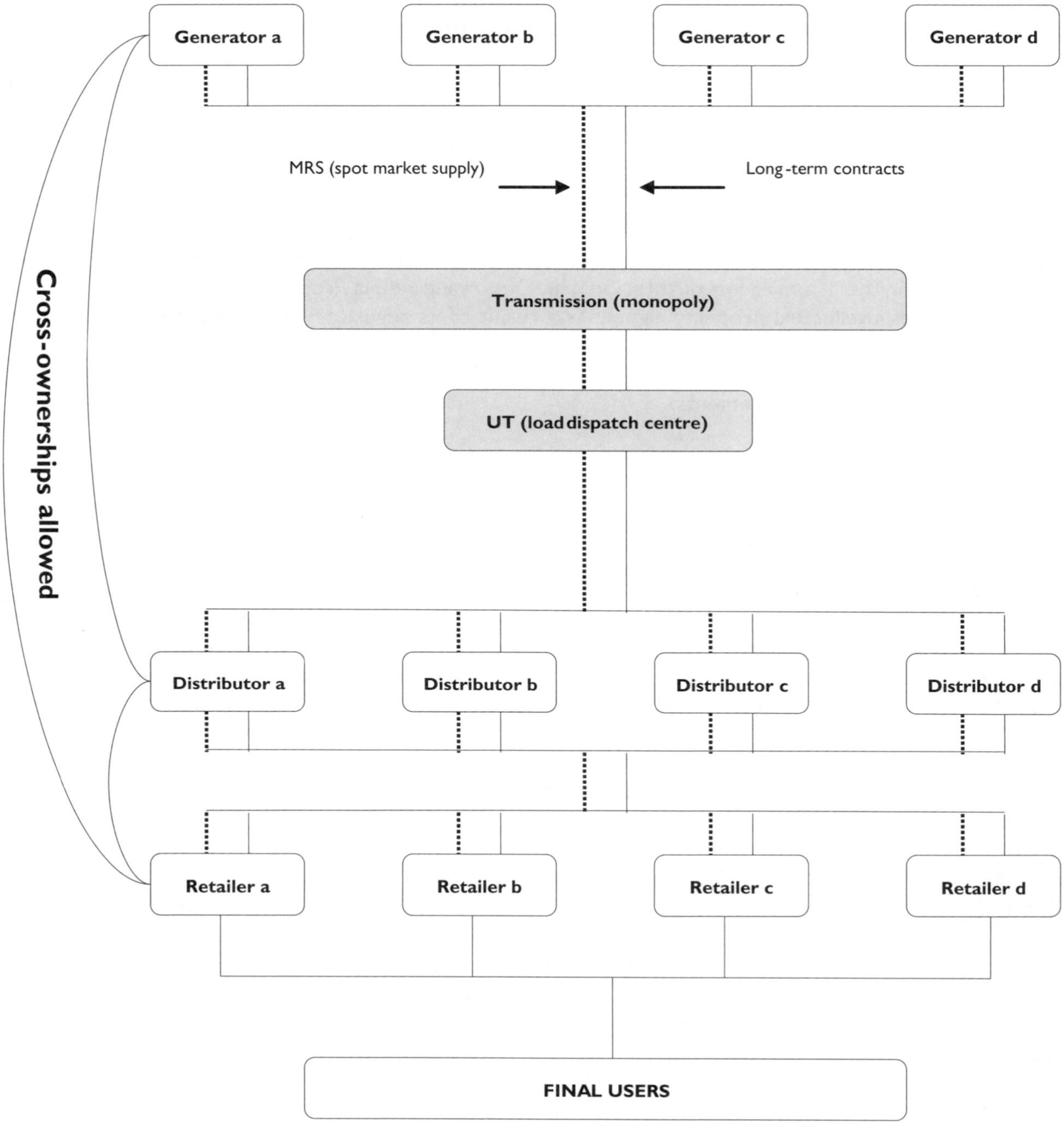

Source: UNCTAD.

The industry has been vertically disaggregated into generation, transmission, distribution and retail. While much of the sector was privatized (chapter I), the government retained ownership in CEL, which operates the hydroelectric plants, and in the transmission company. By law, however, concessions may be granted to private investors for the construction of new hydroelectric power stations, as well as for geothermal plants. For all other power plants,[86] El Salvador adopted a liberal approach that merely requires registration with SIGET.[87] Investors are thus granted total independence in framing their projects, which are not required to conform with a national master plan for development of power plants.

Although the law leaves the door open to private investment in transmission, the sector remains under public ownership. In contrast, the distribution network has been fully privatized and is currently operated by foreign investors (chapter I). Unlike in most other countries, distribution is not a local monopoly, and investors are allowed to set up new distribution networks in areas already served by a competitor. All distribution companies, however, are required to authorize access to their networks to retailers, at a cost regulated by SIGET.

With this framework, El Salvador has succeeded in introducing competition in the key segments of the market, i.e. generation and retail, while imposing well-crafted regulated charges for transmission and distribution services. While other countries with similar frameworks ban certain forms of cross-ownerships, in particular between generators and distributors, El Salvador opted to allow cross-ownership of generators, distributors and retailers, subject to certain rules and regulations, including separate bookkeeping and open access to the distribution lines under regulated charges.

Generators, distributors and retailers set their power supply agreements under freely negotiated terms. In 2007, however, the law was amended to require providers of electricity to final users (whether a distribution company or a retailer) to secure a minimum of 50 per cent of their peak sales through long-term contracts with generators. This amendment was intended to reduce the reliance on the spot market and to foster investment in generation.

The spot market or MRS (Mercado Regulador del Sistema) is operated by the Unidad de Transaciones (UT), which operates as the load-dispatch centre. The UT is an independent entity owned by companies operating in generation, transmission, distribution and retail. Its board includes representatives from the four segments mentioned above, the National Council on Energy, and the Consumer Protection Agency. The UT issues its own regulations on the operation of the transmission system and the MRS. By law, it is required to ensure that electricity demand is satisfied at the lowest cost. The load-dispatch rule currently used on the MRS is based on cost declarations by generators.

The carefully implemented and well-crafted regulatory framework has enabled El Salvador to transition smoothly from a vertically integrated public monopoly to a segmented competitive framework. As illustrated in Chapter I, El Salvador has also succeeded in attracting significant foreign investment by some of the major international players, including AES and Duke. Building on this strong track record, El Salvador has the potential to attract higher levels of FDI in the sector.

While no major regulatory or structural changes are necessary, it is essential that El Salvador continue to build capacity within SIGET and the Superintendence of Competition to monitor practices and ensure that generators and distributors/retailers do not abuse their potential market power, particularly the companies that combine both activities. In addition, El Salvador needs to ensure that the environmental permitting process for new power plants operates efficiently, in order not to lose the benefit of allowing investment in generation without the requirement to obtain a concession.

---

[86] With the exception of nuclear power plants, which are subject to a specific law.

[87] Although concessions are not needed to build thermal power plants, other permitting – in particular environmental permitting – is obviously required.

At the moment, El Salvador relies almost entirely on market forces to ensure that new generating capacity is brought on stream. While this has worked so far, and a number of private investments in generation are planned, it might be useful for El Salvador to prepare an indicative electricity Master Plan providing medium- and long-term demand forecasts and highlighting the areas where investment in generation, transmission and distribution are most needed. A Master Plan would be useful to promote the energy mix that El Salvador wishes to achieve, particularly as it pertains to the development of renewable sources of electricity and efforts to minimize environmental impacts, including in terms of CO_2 emission.[88] This could also help private investors identify business opportunities, and would support PROESA in its investment promotion activities in the sector.

A competitive framework was introduced in telecommunications even faster than in electricity. The technical and regulatory challenges are smaller in the former, and the Law on Telecommunications introduced an appropriate legal framework for the development of mobile and fixed telephony, internet services and long-distance calls, which are crucial for businesses and foreign investors. The telecommunication sector has developed rapidly since it was liberalized in the mid-1990s, including through the participation of foreign investors (chapter I).

El Salvador has opted for a light-handed approach in authorizing companies to operate in telecommunications, and it does not impose any restriction on foreign ownership. Similarly to the electricity sector, many services do not require a concession from SIGET and are subject to a simple registration procedure.[89] In order to foster competition, however, the law imposes various requirements on operators, particularly in terms of interconnectivity.

As illustrated by the rapid development of the sector and the prevailing competitive conditions, the regulatory and supervisory framework is strong. The most important element, in this context, is for SIGET to continue to reinforce its cooperation with the Superintendence of Competition to ensure that the competitive framework is fully implemented in practice and that low-cost and high-quality services are offered to the public at large and to local businesses.

b. Higher education

The higher education system plays a fundamental role in allowing Salvadoreans to secure good job opportunities at home and in providing the necessary skills for the economy to develop and for firms to be competitive. Public investment, appropriate regulations and proactive policies are essential to creating a high-quality education system. Private investment and FDI, however, can also make a significant contribution. Chapter III, section B.1, of this review considers regulatory and strategic aspects in view of leveraging FDI for skills development.

c. Capital markets

The establishment of an efficient capital market would be essential to improve financial intermediation and promote investment by national and foreign companies alike. Chapter III, section B.3 discusses the role that FDI could play in developing thriving capital markets in El Salvador, including in terms of the regulatory reforms needed.

---

[88] In the United Kingdom, which also relies on market forces for the development of new generating capacity, National Grid – the private company that owns and operates the transmission network – recently called on the authorities to develop a nationwide Energy Master Plan to meet the climate-change challenge.

[89] The use of the electromagnetic spectrum is obviously subject to strict regulations and is allocated on the basis of concessions.

D. Assessment and recommendations

El Salvador's regulatory framework reflects the country's firm strategic choice to develop as an open market economy. Great progress has been achieved over the past decade, not only to put in place the laws and regulations necessary to operate a market economy efficiently, fairly and in accordance with development objectives, but also to establish the supporting regulatory and oversight institutions. In this context, the establishment of the Superintendence of Competition, the Consumer Protection Agency, SIGET, and the adoption of a law on the environment are notable accomplishments.

Nonetheless, important economic, social and development challenges remain. Much progress needs to be made in fighting poverty and income inequality. Education indicators are not satisfactory, and threats to personal safety are uncomfortably high. On the economic front, El Salvador faces internal and external challenges, including the need to further increase competitiveness, move up the value chain and adapt the tax regime for the maquila sector in the context of the WTO rules.

On the basis of these challenges, and given the need for El Salvador to enable locally established companies to achieve regional and global competitiveness, a number of recommendations related to FDI are suggested below. The authorities should act on regulatory aspects in three main priority areas, with the objective of achieving global or regional excellence: (a) the general framework; (b) human capital; and (c) infrastructure.

El Salvador should aim to achieve global excellence in the general framework for investment, both as it affects foreign investors and as it affects national investors. Care will need to be taken in terms of the adequacy of laws and regulations as well as the effective implementation and administration of rules. The key actions identified in this chapter are to:

- Review corporate taxation in view of the need bring tax incentives for EPZs in compliance with WTO regulations by 2015, and in order to address the low level of tax revenue;

- Bring the customs office to global standards of excellence, and improve trade facilitation functions;

- Support the work of the Superintendence of Competition;

- Promote environmentally sustainable development;

- Improve or clarify certain provisions specific to foreign investors; and

- Ensure an effective implementation and administration of laws and regulations. The Government should continue to invest in building capacity in key regulatory agencies such as SIGET, the Superintendence of Competition, and the upcoming unified banking and financial markets regulatory authority.

Efforts to build skills and human capital could be improved by implementing a new approach to the allocation of work permits for foreigners, inspired by the H1-B visa system in the United States. In terms of infrastructure, El Salvador should strengthen and widen its efforts to attract first-class foreign investors. Building on the experience it has gained in electricity and telecommunications, the country should also seek to use FDI to develop a high-quality port infrastructure and further extend the network of roads (chapter III).

III. FDI AS A CATALYST FOR NATIONAL COMPETITIVENESS AND SUSTAINABLE DEVELOPMENT

A. Introduction

El Salvador aspires to significantly raise the standards of living of its population and make a sharp dent in poverty and inequality. With a per capita gross national income of $3,480,[90] the country was ranked ninety-second in the world in 2008, at the high end of the lower middle-income countries. Rising to the high end of the upper middle-income group of countries[91] will be a steep and demanding climb. Few non-oil-producing economies have achieved or surpassed this in the last quarter-century, with Hong Kong (China), Singapore, the Republic of Korea and Taiwan Province of China as the most notable exceptions. In Latin America, only Chile and Mexico are near the $10,000 mark.[92]

As a small country and economy, El Salvador has done relatively well so far in breaking its size constraint on FDI attraction.[93] As highlighted in chapter II, it made a firm and resolute choice to adopt an open and outward-oriented development strategy; being the first Central American signatory to bring CAFTA-DR into force symbolizes this proactive stance. When the partnership agreement with the European Union is in place, the key platforms for El Salvador to trade globally on favourable terms will be further consolidated.

Achieving duty-free access to the rich economies of North America and Europe is a crucial step. Translating trade opportunities into sustainable development, poverty reduction and wide opportunities for decent work,[94] however, requires measures to bring skills, infrastructure, public administration and domestic enterprises to globally competitive levels. This is the key challenge for most middle-income countries, which inevitably lose competitiveness in low-cost labour-intensive industries to lower-income economies. It is also what enables countries to move up the value chain and produce more diversified goods and services with higher local value addition and national linkages.

FDI is in a position to make a significant contribution to meeting this challenge and to realizing El Salvador's development objectives, but supportive and proactive policies are required. Chapter II offers concrete recommendations on how to achieve global excellence in the regulatory framework and public administration for investment, with a view to fostering national and foreign investment. This chapter offers further suggestions about strategies to promote the catalytic role of FDI on two main fronts:

- **Supporting competitiveness:** A strategy is proposed to enhance the benefits of FDI on skills, infrastructure and capital markets development and its catalytic role on the internationalization of national enterprises.

- **Fostering environmentally and socially sustainable development**, including through the creation of decent work opportunities: a general strategy is complemented by selected sectoral recommendations.

The implications of these strategies in terms of investment promotion, and for the work of PROESA, are analysed. The need for a small economy like El Salvador to attract niche investors is considered too, as part of the limitations of sectoral targeting.

---

[90] As per the World Bank's Atlas method. The method does not adjust for purchasing power parity, but converts national currency figures into dollars using an inflation-adjusted three-year moving average exchange rate.

[91] The World Bank classifies lower middle-income countries as those with a per capita gross national income of between $976 and $3,855. Upper middle-income countries are those in the $3,856 to $11,905 range.

[92] The Bolivarian Republic of Venezuela is almost at $10,000 as well, but is highly dependent on oil.

[93] UNCTAD (forthcoming, a) provides policy lessons on how to attract and benefit from FDI in small countries, building on the case studies of Estonia and Jamaica.

[94] The International Labour Organization put forward the concept of "decent work", which encompasses income, rights, voice and recognition, family stability and personal development, fairness and gender equality.

B. FDI in support of national competitiveness

Developing countries are frequently confronted with skills and infrastructure deficiencies. Growth in certain countries or regions often outpaces the necessary investments in infrastructure and skills to support economic activity, competitiveness and a rising population, because such investments require long-term planning and implementation, in addition to major expenditures. In other cases, infrastructure and skills development may be lacking, as a result of insufficient funds for public investment.

Regardless of the causes, bottlenecks to economic development emerge, which become highly visible when manifested in congested ports and transport systems or electricity blackouts and brownouts. Bottlenecks and hurdles to competitiveness may be less visible but are no less real when skills development fails to keep up with the needs of the economy, usually as a result of insufficient investment in higher education and vocational training. Similarly, the economy as a whole may be pulled back if local small and medium-sized enterprises (SMEs) do not develop towards international standards of competitiveness and if capital markets do not allow an effective financial intermediation and access to funds.

I. Leveraging FDI for skills development

The level of skills of the population – the nation's human capital – is not only a key determinant of economic development, competitiveness and FDI attraction, but also a fundamental element of human development and access to opportunities for decent work. Increasing the level of skills plays an essential role in improving productivity, and hence in raising per capita incomes.

The primary responsibility for skills development rests with the national education system, which relies on public investment. As it currently stands, El Salvador does not perform very strongly on education indicators when compared with other countries in the region or at a similar level of economic development (chapter I). Public investment in education is relatively low by international standards, and the country's educational outputs are outpaced by the skills demands to increase competitiveness.

The private sector regularly points out that the general level of training is insufficient and that the country suffers from skills shortages. The inadequate knowledge of English of the population at large is particularly problematic in a country that is widely oriented towards the North American market. Proficiency in English is essential in order to attract export-oriented investments and to create jobs with an international dimension. Call centres and other e-enabled services, tourism and commercial professions, for example, are among the sectors that are most dependent on a knowledge of English for their development. In spite of these shortcomings, however, private investors widely recognize that the Salvadorean workforce is one of the country's strongest assets, as it is regarded as being committed and professional and having a good ability to learn.

The authorities are conscious of these deficiencies and needs. The National Education Plan 2021[95] establishes four main objectives (11 years of basic education for all, integral personal development, technical and technological training, and science and technology development) and four main implementation strategies with intermediate goals (access to education, effective basic education, competitiveness in education, and good management practices in education). The necessity to generalize English as a second language as an element of competitiveness, openness to the world, and access to information and technology, is explicitly recognized and given emphasis. So far, however, El Salvador has been confronted with the difficulty of finding qualified teachers.[96]

---

[95] Plan Nacional de Educación 2021. Metas y políticas para construir el país que queremos.

[96] The Government has begun training English-language teachers with the assistance of the American School in San Salvador, and aims to have at least one qualified teacher in each school. So far there are 2,000 teachers with diplomas from the American School, but there are 5,300 schools, so there is a long way to go.

While public investment in education will remain the single most important driver in building human capital, private investment and FDI can also make a significant contribution. As indicated below, private national investment in higher education is already sizeable in El Salvador. So far, however, the Government has not genuinely analysed the specific contribution that FDI could make, in particular in terms of higher education and vocational training. This aspect is not considered in Plan 2021, and foreign investors in education are not targeted by PROESA.

The sections below seek to fill this gap. International trends and practices in FDI in education are considered first, followed by an evaluation of the regulatory framework for higher education. Concrete strategic and regulatory recommendations are then provided.

a.   International trends and practices

There has been a strong worldwide increase in demand for higher education in recent years, with a growing response in terms of cross-border provision of educational services. Much of this has taken the form of universities and institutes taking foreigners on their existing campuses, which requires students to travel abroad. The United States, the United Kingdom, France, Germany and Australia are the top countries attracting foreign students. These represent more than 10 per cent of the total student body (table III.1) in all the aforementioned countries except the United States. Foreign students generate significant local spending, and it is estimated that they contributed $15 billion to the United States economy in 2008. Student mobility between developing countries has been more limited so far, even though it, too, is increasing.[97]

Table III.1. Top countries of destination for foreign students[1]

Country	Number of foreign students	Foreign students (percentage of national total)
United States	623 805	3.5
United Kingdom	389 330	16.3
France	266 448	11.9
Germany	233 606	12.0
Australia	223 508	22.5
China	195 503	..
Canada	123 901	7.4
Japan	123 829	3.0

[1] 2008 or most recent year available.

Source: Institute of International Education, Atlas of Student Mobility.

In addition, however, universities have increased their presence abroad through collaboration programmes under a variety of arrangements. More recently, certain developing countries have sought to raise their domestic capacity by encouraging foreign institutions to establish locally (box III.1).

Table III.2 summarizes the principal modes of supply of education services by foreign universities, based on the case of business management education. All modes have their place in supporting educational progress. The most sustained form of commitment is the joint venture/subsidiary model, which is a form of FDI. China, Malaysia and Singapore have been pioneers in soliciting this form of FDI, and other countries have followed suit.

---

[97] India attracted around 19,000 foreign students in 2007. Malaysia hosts 25,000; South Africa 54,000; and Mexico 3,000.

Box III.1. Examples of FDI ventures and foreign investors in education

In **Singapore**, INSEAD, a leading European business school, set up an Asian campus in 2000. In addition, Cornell University's well-known School of Hotel Administration jointly owns and operates the Cornell-Nanyang Institute of Hospitality Management in Nanyang Technological University's Business School. Both are examples of striving to attract world-class institutions in specialized fields.

Malaysia has been encouraging FDI in education since 1996. There are now five foreign universities with branches in the country and 600 private colleges offering local and foreign qualifications. 34 per cent of all undergraduate and graduate programmes are offered by foreign institutions. Malaysia now has 25,000 fee-paying foreign students, principally from the region.

China has a number of foreign universities, including the Johns Hopkins University–Nanjing University Centre for Chinese and American Studies, the Ningbo campus of the University of Nottingham, and the Xi'an Jiaotong–Liverpool University (XJTLU), which were opened in 1986, 2005 and 2006, respectively. Johns Hopkins is a leading university in the United States, and the United Kingdom parent universities of the latter two are members of the Russell Group of leading British universities. XJTLU students undertake a British degree programme, and all students study English on campus for the first two years. XJTLU is situated in the Suzhou Industrial Park near Shanghai, alongside many TNCs, and the land and buildings are an investment by the park owner. Laureate Education, a private educational investor, is also involved.

In **Viet Nam**, Australia's Royal Melbourne Institute of Technology opened a campus in Ho Chi Minh City in 2001, and a second campus in Hanoi in 2004. It currently has around 4,000 degree students, including in commerce and IT programmes, in addition to 2,000 "academic English" students. It also offers graduate business management programmes. All courses are in English, and the academic English programme is designed to prepare students for study in English. The campuses are fully foreign-owned.

Dubai set up the Knowledge Village in 2003 as a human resources management hub. It is set up as an "education free-trade zone", where professional training and linguistic centres, human resources consultancies and other knowledge-oriented institutions enjoy tax-free treatment. It was founded "as part of a long-term economic strategy to develop the region's talent pool and accelerate its move into a knowledge-based economy."

In most countries, higher education has been sponsored by the state or by specialized non-profit organizations. **For-profit institutions**, however, are emerging to invest across borders. Two significant players are Apollo Inc and Laureate Education Inc, both based in the United States.

Apollo was a pioneer in accessible higher education for working students, and has developed many campuses in the United States since 1976. It has extensive collaborative programmes with universities worldwide. In 2007, Apollo Global was formed as a $1 billion joint venture with the private equity group Carlyle, as a vehicle to invest outside of the United States. Apollo Global acquired the University of Arts, Sciences and Communication in **Chile** and a 65 per cent equity interest in the Latin American University in **Mexico** in 2008.

Laureate Education owns universities in the United States and has partnerships with at least 40 universities around the world, including several in Central America. It has purchased the whole or part of private higher education institutions in **Chile** and **Mexico** and recently acquired *Universidad Interamericana*, a university with campuses in **Costa Rica** and **Panama**. It specializes in a form of franchising – for example, it is opening "learning centres" in **Bahrain**, **Egypt**, **Qatar** and the **United Arab Emirates**, with local investors.

Sources: UNCTAD and universities' websites.

Table III.2. Management education, modes of supply by foreign universities[1]

Supply mode	Nature of education activity	Significance for the country
Admission of foreign students on home campus	Education is provided at the University's home campus. Foreign students are integrated in regular programmes of study.	• Students obtain a degree in a foreign institution and are exposed to foreign languages and culture. • Costs can be high for the student and his/her family. • Student may decide not to return to the home country at the end of the programme. • Spillovers are limited for the country as a whole. • Number of students going abroad is bound to be limited.
Distance learning	Distance learning products differentiated by: • Provision of learning material: Hard copy, e-learning. • Lecturer/tutor support: None, local support, staff support from foreign universities. • Degree award: Host country university, foreign university, joint degree.	• Variability in quality of foreign providers, and potential for deceit. • Introduces new knowledge and thinking, learning methods, books and material. • Opportunities for fairly large-scale provision in future to meet unsatisfied demand for higher education. • Inadequacy of essential services and infrastructure.
Collaboration with local universities	Range of association / partnership agreements, of greater or lesser commitment. Greater commitment associated with classes taught by foreign professors, similar curricula and books, degrees awarded by overseas partner or jointly.	• Many different types of arrangements. • Strong commitment by foreign universities desirable, combined with training of local staff. • Introduction of interactive teaching methods important. • Greater localization desirable e.g. local case studies. • Joint degrees and dual-country study offer major multicultural benefits.
Joint ventures and wholly-owned subsidiaries	Differentiated from collaboration mode by establishment of campuses in host country. Greater degree of commitment extending for example to training of host country faculty abroad or writing of case studies for the host country. Some joint ventures established by intergovernmental agreements e.g. between foreign university (acting on behalf of the foreign Government) and host country Government.	• Similar advantages as advanced collaboration. • Resident foreign staff may increase spillover benefits. • Leads to opportunities for student (and staff) exchanges.

[1] *Relates primarily to MBAs and management master's degrees, mainly in Western universities.*
Source: UNCTAD.

In El Salvador, the joint venture/subsidiary model could be proactively promoted in order to foster enhancements of higher education in several ways. One is adopting international standards of quality and pedagogy in tertiary education. Another is bringing in specialized professional and technical training institutes. The aim of these efforts should be to impart the highest global training standards. For example, the tourism industry would benefit from the establishment of a leading hotel school either from a United States university (such as Cornell) or a highly rated Swiss hotel school.

The aforementioned examples are not only about providing training for nationals, but also about setting quality benchmarks for local institutions. FDI in higher education could also help in increasing the offer in essential areas of education, for example English language training. Achieving such outcomes, however, would require proactive policies to be put in place and regulatory reforms to be adopted. These are the subject of sections b and c below.

b.   The regulatory framework in higher education

The central role of education in human, social and economic development is explicitly recognized in the Constitution: access to education is a constitutional right, and elementary schooling is free[98] and compulsory. In addition, the Constitution guarantees the right of individuals and legal entities (i.e. private investors, both national and foreign) to establish private teaching centres at all levels of education.

---

[98] If provided by public schools.

The first private university[99] was established in 1965 by Jesuits under the Law on Private Universities.[100] Three more private universities were created in the 1970s, reflecting the confrontation between conservative and liberal ideologies. The number of private universities surged during the civil war in the 1980s and early 1990s. By the time legal reforms were first introduced under the Law on Higher Education[101] of 1995, El Salvador had 41 universities (1 public and 40 private), which together with their regional branches and specialized or technological institutes represented 112 higher education centres, for a population of less than 6 million people. Few quality controls were enforced, and the overall quality of education was mediocre.

The Law on Higher Education of 1995 introduced more stringent requirements on private universities, which were further reinforced under the Law on Higher Education of 2004. As a result, a number of private universities were forced to close. As of 2008, however, El Salvador still had 24 universities, with a total student population of 127,685.[102] On average, universities have around 5,300 students, and seven of them have fewer than 1,000. In addition, there are currently 14 specialized and technological institutes, all but three of them with fewer than 1,000 students.

The Law on Higher Education of 2004 explicitly stipulates that foreign education institutions are allowed to open centres in El Salvador and that they are subject to the same regulations and requirements as national institutions. Cooperation agreements with local universities are allowed too, subject to approval by the Ministry of Education.

Private and public universities are free of academic, financial or management interference by the Government. Private universities may only be established as not-for-profit organizations, however, and all net income must be reinvested in research, teaching or infrastructure. The more stringent requirements imposed by the 2004 Law on Education oblige universities to:

- Offer programmes in at least five different fields, covering sciences, humanities and technical areas;
- Conduct research in the fields covered;
- Provide adequate infrastructure (library, classrooms, laboratories and other facilities); and
- Have at least one academic for 40 students.

In order to contain the plethora of universities, the law subjects the creation of any new centre to the approval of the Ministry of Education, after non-binding advice from the Council of Higher Education.[103] In addition to the business plan, candidates must justify how the new university would respond to an objective need of the country. The Council of Higher Education comprises 10 members: two from the Ministry of Education, six from existing universities or specialized centres, and two from the business sector.

In addition to imposing more stringent formal requirements, the Law on Higher Education of 2004 sought to increase the quality of universities by improving the monitoring system, which is currently based on three levels:

- **Grading** is a statistical tool that monitors universities on more than a dozen indicators, including the number of students per professor, the number of full-time vs. part-time academics, the number of computers per student, the cost per academic year etc. Grading is compulsory and results are published every year.

---

[99] Universidad Centroamericana José Simeón Cañas.
[100] Ley de Universidades Privadas.
[101] Ley de Educación Superior.
[102] The single public university, Universidad de El Salvador, has 40,000 students – almost a third of the entire student population.
[103] Consejo de Educación Superior.

- **Evaluation** must be carried out at least every three years, and is based on an auto-evaluation and an external assessment. It is based on more qualitative aspects than the grading system, such as governance, research, or programmes of studies.

- **Certification** is conducted on a voluntary basis and involves more stringent requirements. Certification is granted by a special commission,[104] comprising academics who are not affiliated with any university and who are appointed by mutual agreement between the Ministry of Education and the Council of Higher Education. Accreditation can be granted for a university as a whole or for a specific programme. It is based on an evaluation that examines – among other things – institutional integrity, the academic body, programmes of study, research, and infrastructure. Of the 38 universities and specialized or technical institutes, only 13 were accredited in 2008.

c. A strategy of FDI in education

In spite of its openness to FDI in higher education, El Salvador has so far not attracted foreign universities or technical schools. This is partly for lack of proactive promotion and targeting of foreign educational institutions, but it is also the consequence of regulatory issues. FDI in higher education has the potential to improve the competitiveness of the economy as a whole and make the country more attractive to investors. In addition, it could yield a variety of specific benefits, including: higher quality standards; access to knowledge and know-how; improved training of students and exposure to multiculturalism; spillover effects; mobility of professors and students; and improved capacity for R&D.

It is, therefore, strongly recommended that El Salvador make the attraction of FDI in higher education and vocational training a top priority. A dialogue should be initiated rapidly with all stakeholders, in particular higher education institutions, academia and student representatives. Regulatory and policy recommendations are provided below in order to implement a strategy of FDI attraction in higher education.

Regulatory measures

- **Remove potential regulatory hurdles to FDI**: Two legal requirements on allowing new universities could constitute barriers to FDI in higher education: (a) that candidates offer programmes in at least five different fields; and (b) that the new university correspond to an "objective need of the country". The first requirement should be qualified to allow internationally recognized universities to establish specialized schools in El Salvador, without being required to cover a minimum of five fields of study.[105] In addition, the Ministry of Education should apply the "objective need" criterion with flexibility and the understanding that reputable foreign universities may bring particular benefits to El Salvador.

- **Strengthen compulsory quality controls**: The stricter requirements imposed on all universities in 1995 and 2004 cut the excessive number of centres of higher education and improved quality. The average size of universities remains too small, however, to reach economies of scale, to conduct research and investigation, and to guarantee the quality of education that students deserve. El Salvador should consider making accreditation compulsory for all universities and specialized or technical schools.

In addition, quality assurance is an essential regulatory issue in cross-border education. It is less likely to be an issue if internationally reputed institutions establish subsidiaries in El Salvador,

---

[104] Comisión de Acreditación de la Calidad de la Educación Superior.

[105] Internationally recognized universities have increasingly opened specialized schools overseas, such as the INSEAD MBA programme in Singapore, and the Chinese and American Studies Centre of the Johns Hopkins University in Nanjing. These tend to be highly specialized programmes, however, which cover only one field of study and would thus not be allowed by the current regulations in El Salvador.

but it is important to protect local students against potentially substandard courses delivered by foreign providers, including through distance learning. Quality assurances are important not only for universities, but also for technical, vocational and language schools.

- **Establish intermediate schools and degrees**: The centres that do not qualify for full-fledged university status could apply to become specialized schools, vocational schools, or the equivalent of community or junior colleges in the United States. The latter offer intermediate degrees and provide a cheaper alternative to colleges offering four-year bachelor's degrees. They lead to an associate degree after a two-year programme, which can also be used as a stepping stone to enter the third year of a bachelor's degree in a college or university. Programmes such as legal assistant, technician or IT specialist would be excellent candidates for such degrees, potentially opening the path to law, engineering or computer programming degrees.

Policy and institutional measures

- **Join the Bologna Process (Bologna Policy Forum)**: Twenty-nine European countries adopted the Bologna Declaration on the European Higher Education Area in 1999, with the purpose of making degrees comparable and recognized throughout the area, establishing a common system of credits, promoting quality assurance, and fostering the mobility of students, teachers and researchers. The process has been extremely successful and 46 countries have now joined the process in a pan-European area. In addition, 15 non-European countries[106] joined the Bologna Policy Forum, which seeks to promote cooperation with the members of the European Higher Education Area in terms of mutual recognition of degrees, mobility of students and academics, and quality assurance. El Salvador could benefit greatly from joining the Bologna Policy Forum as a way to improve the quality of its university system and promote mobility of students and academics, in and out of the country.

- **Promote region-wide recognition of qualifications and an education hub**: It would be clearly advantageous to the economy and the national workforce for graduate and technical degrees to gain regional recognition. While some progress has been achieved in that respect through the process of Central American economic integration, much remains to be done. El Salvador could take the lead and entice its regional partners to aim at the creation of a Central American Higher Education Area, set up along the lines of the Bologna Process. It would support the establishment of a regional market for educational services, in which El Salvador could aim to become a hub through its proactive stance and with the help of FDI.

- **Consider the potential role of for-profit institutions**: El Salvador does not currently allow for-profit institutions of education. Such institutions, however, are emerging as significant cross-border investors. It may be worthwhile for the Government to investigate the role that they could play in the country's education system, and whether they could be admitted on a regulated basis. Issues to investigate include the areas in which they would be allowed (e.g. language and technical schools, evening classes or training for company employees), the corporate income tax regime, and the status of partnerships between profit-driven investors and not-for-profit institutions.

- **Build bridges between universities and the private sector**: An effective interface between institutions of higher education and the business community is essential on two main counts. Firstly, it allows the former to adapt curricula to the needs of the economy, and facilitates the entry of students into the job market. Secondly, it allows the establishment of mutually beneficial partnerships, particularly in terms of R&D.

---

[106] These include developing countries such as Brazil, China and Mexico, as well as OECD countries including Australia, Canada and the United States.

A number of initiatives ought to be considered to reinforce that interface. The private sector could be consulted when defining curricula, in particular in technical schools. Representatives from the private sector could be invited as visiting professors, and the Government should encourage companies to offer internships to students by creating a legal status for interns and perhaps exempting employers from social security contributions.

In addition, the consolidation of universities into larger centres of education and the entry of foreign institutions should strengthen the ability of universities to conduct research. This should allow better partnerships with private companies and the establishment of joint ventures. Business clusters have appeared around leading universities around the world, including Silicon Valley and Stanford University in California, the technopole in Cambridge, and R&D projects between TNCs and Tsinghu University in China. In El Salvador, the Government could set up a small incubator fund to promote R&D-based joint ventures between universities and the private sector, and could provide guidelines to help universities define the nature of such joint ventures, particularly as far as intellectual property rights are concerned.

- **Promote wider access to higher education**: At about 139,000, the number of students in higher education is still relatively low in El Salvador. The Government could consider requiring that private universities and specialized schools subsidize the admission of a number of students on a means-tested and merit basis.[107] This would promote access to higher education for qualified students from poorer families.

- **Promote and facilitate access to textbooks and teaching material**: Universities are likely to rely at least partly on international textbooks, in addition to their own teaching material. Some of the benefits of attracting foreign universities lies in the proprietary teaching material that they are likely to use. Being subject to copyrights, however, textbooks tend to be expensive and beyond the budget of many students. The Government could attempt to coordinate bulk purchases of textbooks in order to reduce costs. It could also explore ways to fully exploit limitations and exceptions to copyright laws that are available for textbooks under the TRIPS agreement. UNCTAD could provide technical assistance in that respect.

- **Proactively promote FDI in higher education**: Given the benefits associated with FDI in higher education, PROESA should include the sector as one of its priority areas for targeting and promotion (section D). In this context, PROESA could conduct a market research study to fully understand the potential market and the drivers of FDI in education, and identify targets.

2.   Strengthening infrastructure through FDI

In the same way that FDI in education could contribute to building El Salvador's human capital, foreign investors could play a major role in building the country's backbone infrastructure. Unlike in education, El Salvador has already sought and succeeded in attracting large foreign investments in infrastructure, in particular electricity and telecommunications (chapters I and II). However, the potential for FDI to further build and improve the country's infrastructure is large if additional policies are put in place.

As indicated in chapter I, El Salvador has an unusual mix of good and poor infrastructure, ranging from trunk roads nearly of the standard seen in developed countries, to a single operating international seaport relying on ship cranes for loading and unloading. The trunk network consists mostly of dual carriageway roads that are well maintained. Urban roads are also of a good standard, and San Salvador has some elements of

---

[107] For example, private universities could be required to admit a small percentage of students on the basis of the level of tuition paid to attend the Universidad de El Salvador.

express throughways and a ring road. The road system has been publicly funded, and maintenance, which is often problematic in developing countries, is financed through a special levy on fuel sales.[108]

Little attention has been given so far to private road concessioning. Urban roads, especially in San Salvador, offer interesting possibilities in the form of a ring road and express through-roads, as they have the key characteristics needed for commercial success and community acceptability – they have dense traffic, and existing roads give users reasonable free alternatives. Four potential road concession projects have been identified by the Ministry of Public Works, including two sections of the San Salvador ring road.

Acajutla is currently the only operational port, and its facilities are well below international standards. Construction of a new port in La Unión – on the initiative of the Government – was finalized in 2008. It was intended to be concessioned to a private operator, but has remained idle so far due to political disputes over the terms of the concession (chapter I).

El Salvador liberalized and introduced private investment in the electricity sector early on, and has done very well in establishing a high-quality regulatory framework to introduce competition where feasible (chapter II). Similarly, it liberalized and privatized telecommunications in the 1990s. Since then, foreign investors have become prominent players in both sectors, contributing to the development of the infrastructure (chapter I).

In many areas, El Salvador offers infrastructure that provides good competitive support for businesses to compete regionally or globally. Infrastructure has been built and operated under a judicious mix of public and private investment. There is a welcome absence of telltale signs of systematic breakdown in planning, developing, and operating key infrastructure services, such as electricity blackouts, road congestion or poor road maintenance. The regulation of operations in liberalized markets has been progressive and competent.

As a result, the clearest strategic priority is to improve capacity to introduce private investment in the transport sector. This should commence by restarting the concession of La Unión and then moving to a selective programme of road concessions.

Concessioning La Unión

Completing the concessioning of La Unión to a leading and internationally recognized port operator should be considered as an absolute priority. The port is intended not only to service the import and export needs of El Salvador, but also to attract transhipment business by actively competing with rival logistics centres in the region. This ambition is more likely to be fulfilled by a private operator than by a government operation. Expert advice from investment banking and technical advisers will be needed on:

● The commercial terms and conditions of the concession that are likely to attract private investment while safeguarding the public interest. Chief among the latter are competition aspects, since La Unión will likely become the main port for the domestic market. Consideration should be given to whether Acajutla could be concessioned separately, and also whether separate terminals could be concessioned in La Unión.

● The feasibility of the dry canal and the economic benefits of public expenditure to support high standard overland routes to the Atlantic ports in Honduras and Guatemala.

The failure, so far, to execute a concession for La Unión suggests some valuable lessons if El Salvador is to attract FDI through public–private partnerships (PPP) in transport. La Unión should have been structured

---

[108] In addition, a municipal tax on personal income is levied to finance the extension and maintenance of local roads.

as a PPP project from the outset. This would have enabled the commercial potential to be fully explored, the commercial terms acceptable to private investors and the public interest to be designed, and the political commitment to be secured to them. The terms of such a major project should have been set out in legislation. It should be noted that this disciplined approach would not have precluded government capital contributions if these were in the public interest.

The delays in the La Unión concession raise questions about El Salvador's capacity and commitment to execute PPP projects. As a result, La Unión should be put back on track as a concession before attempting further concessions. This is the immediate priority. Successfully completing the concession of La Unión would also prepare the ground for the future concession of the airport extension. An unsatisfactory outcome with the port, however, would likely lead to scepticism from international investors on the airport.

Private investment in road infrastructure

El Salvador is already highly ranked in Central and South America in road infrastructure. This has been achieved through traditional public works contracting. El Salvador may seem to be an unlikely candidate to initiate PPPs in roads: the road system is already well developed and public works construction and maintenance has worked well. However, there is a strategic opportunity to develop this success into services exports and outward FDI opportunities in PPPs for Salvadorean civil construction, engineering and allied services companies. The opportunity to develop road concessioning expertise could be pursued as follows:[109]

- Concession two sections of the San Salvador ring road as PPP projects.

- Encourage foreign contractors[110] to participate as project sponsors, but ensure that local contractors participate in the bid consortia as owners, construction contractors or operators. This participation will expose the local contracting and engineering industry to the scale and complexity of PPPs, including the financial, legal and commercial issues that differ significantly from public works contracting. Moreover, the local industry will gain experience of operating toll roads, which goes well beyond maintenance issues and is a key part of securing project financing.

- Utilize the domestic market to raise some of the equity and debt capital required. This can include direct Government measures, such as tax relief on equity investment, and ensuring that pension funds, a key source of infrastructure finance, are permitted to subscribe to equities and to infrastructure bonds.

- As part of this process, expose Salvadorean professionals – including financial services, legal, accounting and economic consulting firms – to the complex transactional issues involved in PPPs.

These experiences will help build El Salvador's capability to participate in PPPs in the region, which are likely to increase. This should be seen as an important outward FDI opportunity, which builds on a demonstrated strength of El Salvador.

Peru's experiences are instructive. PPPs in Peruvian roads typically involved local firms in consortia with large foreign contractors and lead investors (such as Brazil's Odebrecht). But progressive local firms are now gaining the confidence to play a larger role in PPPs, although they have yet to bid abroad. Local firms are acting as road operators. Legal firms are capable of handling the complex commercial documentation involved.

---

[109] UNCTAD (2009b) provides extensive policy lessons on how to utilize FDI to improve road infrastructure, building on the case studies of Australia and Peru.

[110] Brazilian, Chilean and Mexican firms are the most likely candidates, rather than large European or United States firms.

3. Establishing a thriving capital market

Putting in place a thriving and efficient capital market should be considered as a top strategic priority for El Salvador. Efficient financial intermediation is essential not only for the development of local enterprises and their internationalization, but also for the attraction of foreign investors, in particular in infrastructure. However, El Salvador, like most countries in the region, suffers from major deficiencies in financial intermediation. Companies have difficulties in obtaining corporate loans (chapter I), mutual funds and venture capital do not exist, and the equity market has become anaemic.

The stock exchange of El Salvador (Bolsa de Valores de El Salvador (BVES)) was established in 1992. It is regulated under the Law on Securities Market of 1994[111] and supervised by the Superintendence of Securities. Although the BVES has a full infrastructure in place, including electronic trading and a centralized custody system, it has failed to develop as a meaningful source of capital for local companies. Market capitalization is thin, at $6.2 billion as at September 2009 – equivalent to less than 30 per cent of GDP (table III.3). A mere 34 companies are listed, virtually all of them in banking, insurance or finance, with the exception of three companies in the electricity sector and one in telecommunications. So far, none of the bigger local industrial or manufacturing companies have issued equity publicly.

Trading volumes on the BVES have fallen dramatically in the past couple of years, with the acquisition of local banks by foreign investors (chapter I). Although the banks remain listed, actively traded equity amounts to next to nothing. In the first nine months of 2009, equity trading represented less than $3 million, compared with $620 million in 2007 when most publicly listed shares of Banco Salvadoreño and Banco Agrícola were acquired by HSBC and Bancolombia respectively. Non-equity trading volumes – in large part Government bonds – also fell in 2009, which led total trading volumes to fall to $1.5 billion in first nine months, compared to $4.5 billion in 2008.

Table III.3. Equity market indicators, 2006–2009

	2006	2007	2008	2009[1]
Market capitalization ($ million)	7 716	6 593	6 774	6 187
Market capitalization (% GDP)	41.4	32.4	30.6	..
Number of listed companies	35	35	37	34
Annual trading volume (shares)	56 724 596	63 483 116	1 480 328	213 154
Annual trading volume ($ million)	196.8	617.7	18.9	2.4
Memorandum:				
Total trading volume on BVES (equity + non-equity, $ million)	6 765.8	5 819.5	4 485.1	1 544.8

[1] Year to end-September.
Source: Superintendencia de Valores.

There are at least three consequences of the underdeveloped capital market. One is that local innovators and entrepreneurs are denied a vital source of risk capital for new ventures and R&D. A second is that the principal "end game" for owners of mature companies is to sell to foreign investors, rather than to grow and internationalize supported by public capital-raising. A thriving capital market helps local companies grow to become regional "hubs" rather than a "spoke" of a global TNC. A third consequence is that the lack of long-term capital hampers private investment in large infrastructure projects.

Addressing the weaknesses in financial intermediation should thus be seen as a priority for El Salvador and considered part of an overall strategy to improve national competitiveness. It is beyond the scope of this

---

[111] Ley del Mercado de Valores.

review to provide a comprehensive capital market development strategy, but a number of recommendations can be provided:

- Establish a national task force to coordinate the preparation of a capital markets development policy. The policy should cover all areas of financial intermediation, from corporate lending to venture capital and private equity firms, mutual funds, pension funds, insurance companies and others. The task force should involve the capital markets' supervisory bodies, the Central Bank, the Ministry of Finance, the Ministry of Economy and the BVES. Relevant stakeholders from the private sector should be regularly consulted and involved in the process. The task force should aim to make its proposal to Cabinet by the end of 2010.

- Complete the merger of the supervisory bodies for banks, pensions and the stock market, and enhance the autonomy of the merged institution, as El Salvador is committed to do under the Letter of Intent of 7 January 2009 with the IMF.

- Listing requirements should be simplified and clarified without compromising protection of investors or minority shareholders, and without compromising the necessary transparency requirements. Listings should be encouraged as a means for local companies to finance investments, and initial public offerings should be eased, as this is a condition for the emergence of venture capital funds.

- The dialogue between the BVES and the regulatory authority should be improved.

- A legal framework for mutual funds and venture capital funds needs to be established.

- Pension funds should be granted more flexibility in investment choices, under continued strict regulatory supervision.

- A dialogue on corporate lending policies and practices should be initiated with the major banks, with the aim of promoting financing for investment and reversing or stopping the declining trend of corporate loans.

- El Salvador successfully built on the Chilean experience when reforming the structure of its electricity sector. A similar process of lesson-learning should take place in preparing the capital markets development policy. Chile has indeed successfully reformed and revitalized its capital market, starting from many conditions that apply to El Salvador today. Market capitalization in Chile was $208 billion as at September 2009, and assets under management by the 64 venture capital and private equity funds (fondos de inversión) were $5.3 billion as at June 2009.[112] As its capital market developed and pension reforms were introduced, Chile was also able to increase the gross national saving rate from 14 per cent of GDP in 1980 to 24 per cent in 2007–2008. An increase in the saving rate could be an additional benefit of developing efficient financial intermediation in El Salvador.[113]

- After the capital markets development policy has been adopted by Cabinet and once regulatory reforms have been implemented, PROESA should seek to attract foreign venture capital funds.

4. Fostering linkages and the internationalization of local companies

The network of local suppliers – in manufacturing as well as in services – and their competitiveness are a major determinant of a country's attractiveness to foreign investors. In the vast majority of cases, TNCs

---

[112] As a point of reference, Chile has a population of 16.8 million people (almost three times that of El Salvador) and a nominal GDP of $169 billion (close to eight times that of El Salvador).

[113] El Salvador's gross national saving rate averaged 12 per cent of GDP in 2000–2008.

do not wish to operate as enclaves and find it more cost-effective to source a significant share of their supplies locally.[114] In addition, sustained contractual links between national companies (including SMEs) and locally established TNCs are one of the major channels through which the economy as a whole can benefit from FDI. Such linkages facilitate the diffusion of information, technology, skills and management practices. They are also opportunities to reinforce the ability of suppliers to become exporters, and eventually to internationalize through outward FDI.

Linkages with foreign investors are qualified as "backward" when they involve firms supplying TNCs under a long-term relationship, and "forward" when local companies purchase goods or services from TNCs.[115] "Horizontal" linkages emerge from interactions between competing local firms and TNCs.

El Salvador's openness to FDI and to international trade means that local companies have been relatively exposed to international competitive pressures and horizontal linkages. It has helped a number of national firms reach good standards of efficiency and competitiveness, including in property development, logistics services and garments. Forward linkages have also been relatively significant in El Salvador, particularly through the numerous United States franchises in retail and fast food.

Backward linkages also exist, but remain insufficiently developed. The Ministry of Economy, with the support of the United Nations Development Programme (UNDP), has established a supplier development programme.[116] It is targeted at micro, small and medium-sized suppliers. It acts upon requests of larger buyers who feel the need to upgrade their suppliers. Direct support is provided to the suppliers, mostly by making a trained external consultant available for a few months. This programme is valuable, but would need to be enhanced in several respects. First, it is mostly focused on the smaller enterprises, and should be widened to larger companies. The level and type of support services offered could vary according to the kind of supplier involved. Second, it should specifically target TNCs on the buyer's end of the linkages programme, as foreign companies are likely to provide greater spillover benefits. Third, it should diversify the type of support offered to suppliers. Fourth, it should entice TNCs to establish their own supplier development and support programmes.

A number of recommendations may thus be offered, building on UNCTAD's experience in developing linkages programmes and on the lessons of the *World Investment Report 2001*[117] and a forthcoming best practices study on linkages.[118] The linkages programme should seek to promote five areas where linkages bring particular benefits: (a) suppliers/buyers identification; (b) transfers of technology; (c) training, including in terms of management practices; (d) information-sharing, including in terms of future orders or technical requirements; and (e) financial support. Government policy and programmes can influence each of these areas to varying degrees. Possible measures include:

- Establishing an information database on linkages opportunities for TNCs (buyers) and suppliers alike. Some countries have pushed this one step further by assisting more directly in matchmaking, e.g. by organizing fairs, exhibitions or conferences.

- Suppliers can be assisted directly under a programme similar to that already in place in El Salvador (i.e. by financing external consultants). Training of suppliers by the TNCs themselves

---

[114] Export processing zones and maquilas, however, have tended to operate as enclaves in many developing countries. Suppliers' contracts between domestic firms and companies operating in the EPZs are frequently limited, thereby generating little impact on the economy, other than job creation.

[115] Linkages occur only under a long-term relationship and cannot emerge from one-off arm's length transactions.

[116] El Salvador Compite, Programa de Desarrollo de Proveedores.

[117] UNCTAD (2001) provides a comprehensive analysis of FDI and backward linkages. It builds on the lessons learned throughout the developing world to provide concrete policy recommendations on how to establish linkages programmes. It can be consulted for more details on Government programmes and third-country experiences.

[118] UNCTAD (forthcoming, b).

may prove even more valuable, however, and lead to more significant spillovers. Some countries provide tax credits proportional to the expenses incurred for the training of suppliers, while others allow excess tax deductions (i.e. expensing beyond 100 per cent of the costs involved).

● Local absorptive capacity should continue to be strengthened, including through the work of the Fundación Empresarial para la Acción Social (FUNDEMAS) and the EMPRETEC programme, which promotes and supports small entrepreneurs through training programmes.

● Significant transfers of technology are unlikely to occur unless local firms have sufficient absorptive capacity. Such capacity could be developed as part of the efforts to strengthen universities and their research programmes, and to team them up with local businesses (section B.1). Encouraging local firms to register intellectual property rights would also put them in a stronger bargaining position when negotiating transfers of technology agreements with foreign firms.

● Although government intervention in the financial relationships between buyers and suppliers is not desirable, the latter may be supported by establishing legal protection against unfair contractual arrangements or mandating reasonable payments times and penalties for delays. In that respect, speedy and efficient court settlements are also essential.

● Ultimately, further technical assistance from UNCTAD should be considered in establishing a full-fledged linkages programme. Such programmes have been established successfully so far in a number of countries, including Brazil and Uganda, and implementation has started in Argentina, the Dominican Republic and Peru.

● A holistic approach to linkages and supplier development programmes also requires that PROESA pay attention in investor targeting to attracting TNCs that have a strongly developed philosophy and capability for implementing such programmes in host countries. It may also call on PROESA to strengthen aftercare, as this is one of the key instruments to maximize the impact of TNC activities on the economy, either through reinvestments or through increased linkages (section D.4).

In addition to fostering backward linkages between TNCs and local suppliers, the Government may wish to actively promote the internationalization of local firms, as part of its efforts to upgrade the competitiveness of the economy. In the past, outward FDI was often seen in developing countries as a loss of capital, and was discouraged or even prevented by foreign exchange controls. The modern approach is to see outward FDI as helping competitiveness by exposing local companies to international standards.

The facilitation of outward FDI should become a component of the FDI strategy for El Salvador. Outward FDI in the region would be the first step in this process, and a number of Salvadorean companies have already started to invest abroad, in particular in manufacturing and commercial property development. Supporting policy measures need to be in place including:

● Ensuring that double taxation treaties support outward FDI as well as inward FDI (chapter II).

● Developing the capital market so as to fund outward FDI by local companies.

● For manufacturing, in particular, ensuring that logistics and border control mechanisms facilitate the movement of inputs within regional supply chains (chapter II).

C. FDI for sustainable development

The key goals of PROESA in terms of FDI are the following: (a) promote export-oriented investments; (b) diversify the economy; (c) increase local value-addition and move up the value chain; (d) participate more actively in global value chains; and (e) promote linkages. These goals are sensible and coherent with El Salvador's small, open economy development strategy (chapter II). As a small but efficient institution, PROESA has, in the past few years, actively and successfully targeted foreign companies in nine key sectors: (a) business process outsourcing; (b) call centres; (c) textile and garments; (d) agro-industry; (e) tourism; (f) aeronautics; (g) electronics; (h) medical devices; and (i) light manufacturing.

Sectoral targeting has limitations, however, particularly in a small economy. Enticing the largest global TNCs to establish production sites is difficult in small countries, and a significant share of FDI is likely to come from smaller niche foreign investors. In addition, it is notoriously hard for governments or investment promotion agencies to identify the strongest and most valuable business opportunities. In addition to well-defined targeting efforts, it is thus essential for El Salvador – and PROESA – also to put in place programmes to make El Salvador an attractive location for investors across all sectors. Competitiveness is a key element, and the contribution of FDI on that issue has been dealt with in section B. The sections below complement the strategy of using FDI to support competitiveness with elements of an FDI strategy to help achieve sustainable development.

The environment of El Salvador is relatively fragile and under stress. Chapter II recommends that a general policy of sustainable development[119] be prepared. Section 1 below considers the role that FDI could play in such a strategy. It focuses on the opportunities that could be generated for El Salvador from the global trend towards higher levels of environmental protection and from greater worldwide efforts to combat climate change. It considers how innovative policies could transform EPZs to help ensure their sustainability in the face of elimination of WTO-incompatible tax incentives, and later on be extended to the economy as a whole. Sections 2 and 3 provide elements of an FDI strategy for agriculture and tourism, which also have a strong bearing on sustainable development.

1. Export processing zones and "green and responsible" FDI

Export processing zones have helped to diversify El Salvador's production and exports away from traditional commodities and to boost employment in manufacturing. There are now 16 zones and around 200 companies operating within them, of which about 70 per cent are textile and garment firms (chapter I). They have been supported by strong fiscal incentives for zone developers and operating enterprises as well as streamlined customs clearance (chapter II).

Recently, the zones have faced two major challenges. First, there are strong competitive pressures from other countries in the region and in Asia with lower labour costs, particularly for basic garment assembly. Second, tax incentives are incompatible with WTO rules on export subsidies (chapter II). El Salvador – like several other developing countries – enjoys a waiver until 2015, but enforcement of the WTO rule will require corporate income tax on zone exports to be harmonized with corporate taxation on domestic sales. This is regarded in many countries as a serious threat to the durability of zone-based investments.

On the other hand, the Salvadorean zones have two key advantages. Firstly, El Salvador is close to the principal export market, the United States. This proximity allows fast reaction times, and it lowers transport costs. In textiles and garments, it enables quick delivery to minimize costly retailer inventories and provides the opportunity to respond to short fashion cycles.[120] Quick delivery is an advantage enjoyed over Asian competitors. In addition, CAFTA-DR provides import duty advantages and more flexible rules of origin.

---

[119] The term "sustainable development" was introduced and defined in 1987 by the Brundtland Report as "development which meets the needs of the present without compromising the ability of future generations to meet their own needs". The term has nowadays taken a strong connotation of environmental sustainability and protection, including as far as climate change is concerned. It also has an important social connotation, including in terms of workers' rights, income inequality and social stability.

[120] For example, an order can be supplied to Chicago from El Salvador in two weeks, versus one month from China.

Secondly, most zones are privately owned and run, which is an important advantage as private owners are likely to be more proactive than government-owned zones in adjusting to the changing economics of labour-intensive manufacturing. Indeed, a number of zone owners and enterprises are making efforts to adjust to competitive threats, with support from PROESA. The adjustments taking place include:

- Full package supply in textiles and garments: The development of integrated supply chains in textiles and garments, including design, is well advanced. It extends beyond fabric manufacture into production of synthetic and cotton yarns. Existing local capacity has been augmented with a recent $50 million investment by Pettenati of Brazil in synthetic yarn production.

  It is estimated that 50 per cent of fabric used in exported garments is now locally manufactured, compared with 40 per cent five years ago. Approximately 30 per cent of the yarn used in export garments is now locally supplied.[121] Guatemala and the United States are other major suppliers and satisfy the CAFTA-DR rules of origin. There is now also a local supplier industry for accessories. An integrated supply chain reinforces El Salvador's advantage of close proximity to the United States market by improving its ability to respond to short fashion cycles. It is also less sensitive to labour-cost competition than maquila-type garment assembly.

- Diversification into non-textile manufacturing and services: The zones are slowly but steadily diversifying into non-textile areas of manufacturing (chapter I). EPZs and services zones are also hosting new industries such as regional logistics and call centres, and other e-enabled services such as business process outsourcing.

In spite of the diversification currently under way, threats to the competitiveness of EPZ-based enterprises remain. There are question marks about the durability of certain investments once tax incentives are removed as per the WTO requirements, by 2015 at the latest. International competition to attract FDI in manufacturing and services for exports is intense, and the Salvadorean zones need to develop a more distinctive profile to give them a competitive edge while adjusting to the WTO requirements. In this respect, two global developments are working in El Salvador's favour and should be incorporated into an FDI strategy:

- **Environmental issues:** The pressure and international commitment to address global environmental issues – climate change in particular – have increased steadily over the past decade, from the 1992 United Nations Conference on Environment and Development in Rio de Janeiro (Earth Summit) to the Kyoto Protocol under the United Nations Framework Convention on Climate Change (UNFCCC) and the Copenhagen conference in December 2009. Concrete commitments and actions to reduce greenhouse gases have become more prevalent over the past decade, and the trend is likely to continue, whether on a multilateral and binding basis or on a voluntary basis.

  CAFTA-DR has a chapter on the environment, and it established a parallel Environmental Cooperation Agreement (ECA). CAFTA-DR and the ECA do not set environmental regulations, but commit the parties to upholding their national environmental laws in an efficient and transparent manner. Under the treaty's Environmental Affairs Council, a Secretariat of Environmental Affairs has been formed to deal with complaints from any party or member of the public. The ECA encourages the parties to improve national environmental standards and their enforcement, and to develop best environmental practices, including the adoption of technologies for cleaner production techniques.

---

[121] Figures based on UNCTAD interview with the Textile and Apparel Industry Chamber of El Salvador (CAMTEX).

- The prospects of TNCs developing supply chains closer to the major markets due to "green" and climate-change issues has become a reality. Up to 70 per cent of a manufacturer's carbon footprint arises from transport and other transactions in the supply chain.[122] In addition, rising fuel prices have significantly affected transport costs, which gives an edge to producers located close to market.[123] One regional example is a shift by Boeing to make more use of Mexican aerospace suppliers.

   In addition, consumers in key OECD markets have become increasingly sensitive to the environmental impacts involved in the products they purchase. This is illustrated in the high-growth in bio products in most developed economies.

- **Social, labour and corporate social responsibility issues:** Pressed by consumers and advocacy groups, TNCs have paid increasing attention to social and labour practices along their entire supply chain. Virtually all global companies nowadays pay at least lip service to corporate social responsibility (CSR). Many have put in place genuine and *bona fide* corporate social responsibility programmes and use these as a marketing tool.

   In 2000, the United Nations launched the Global Compact as a policy platform and a practical framework to promote sustainable and responsible business practices. Its purpose is to entice corporations to adhere to 10 principles affecting human rights, labour, the environment and anti-corruption, and to make them an integral part of business strategy and day-to-day operations. As of late 2009, more than 5,200 corporations had signed up to the Global Compact, including almost 170 companies from the Financial Times 500 list of the world's largest TNCs by market capitalization. In the United States alone, about 360 companies signed up.[124]

El Salvador could turn these global developments, which could be seen as a constraint, into an opportunity to develop a clear and distinctive profile for its zones. If successful, the policy could be extended nationwide to build a unique profile for the country and for FDI attraction. Such a policy would build on and complement the sustainable development policy as recommended in chapter II.

In several ways, El Salvador is already well positioned to adopt such a strategy. It has made strong progress in recent years in implementing sensible environmental protection regulations (chapter II) and it has actively promoted good practices in corporate social responsibility through the Programa Empresa Salvadoreña para la Responsabilidad Social (EMPRESAL). Several of the EPZs have developed good health centres and labour relations, in addition to making recreational facilities available to workers and their families. Also, labour relations are generally good across the country.

The sections below provide initial recommendations on how to design such a strategy of "green and responsible" investment. More detailed analysis and research would be needed to form the basis of an action plan, if the strategy is to be adopted and implemented.

a.   "Greening" measures

A number of measures could be considered to raise the "green" profile of EPZs in El Salvador. Such measures could potentially be extended to the economy at large to give a "green" profile to the country as a whole:

---

[122] Estimate by Ernst and Young, cited in Financial Times. Crisis and climate force supply chain shift. 9 August 2009.

[123] Gerard Kleisterlee, chief executive of Philips, recently stated that "a future where energy is more expensive and less plentifully available will lead to more regional supply chains." As quoted in Financial Times. Crisis and climate force supply chain shift. 9 August 2009.

[124] http://www.unglobalcompact.org

- Increase technical capacity in the Ministry of Environment and Natural Resources to evaluate environmental impact assessments and monitor compliance. This should aim for high international standards.

- Participate fully and constructively in all the environmental initiatives of CAFTA-DR and the CEA, as well as in the UNFCCC and the post-Copenhagen process.

- Promote the use of carbon accounting in El Salvador, using an internationally accepted methodology. It is essential that accurate and recognized measurements of carbon footprint be possible if El Salvador is to attract investors aiming to reduce greenhouse gas emissions, including under the Clean Development Mechanism (CDM) (see below).

- Promote the development of renewable electricity sources through the electricity Master Plan. Producing electricity from carbon-free sources (e.g. geothermal) would allow zone investors to minimize their carbon footprint.

- Support the development of "green" local suppliers to the zones in order to establish complete "green and responsible" supply chains. Training and sensitization could take place in the context of the existing support programmes for SMEs, including EMPRETEC.

- Increase El Salvador's use of the Clean Development Mechanism (CDM) set up as part of the Kyoto Protocol.[125] The Ministry of Environment and Natural Resources – the designated national authority for the CDM – should take the lead in identifying projects suitable as investments under the CDM, in particular in the energy sector but also in industry. Once identified, PROESA could provide support in targeting potential investors in OECD countries.

- Develop full national standards for wastewater, solid waste and clean air to add to the standards for toxic and hazardous waste that have been developed. These should be as stringent as the United States standards.

- Develop a national pollutant release and transfer registry, akin to the Toxic Release Registry in the United States and to what is contemplated under the European Union's Aarhus system.

- Apply national standards and upgraded compliance procedures first to the zones. This will enable the Government to trial the introduction of upgraded national standards and enable a comprehensive clean production programme to be focused on the zones. The clean production programme should include direct government investment or co-investment, and subsidies and/ or tax incentives to assist zone/non-zone businesses to lower energy use, emissions and waste.

- Incorporate the results into country marketing and branding to show El Salvador promoting cutting-edge environmental standards in and out of the export processing zones (section D.1).

- Mandate EXPORTA, the export-promotion agency, to conduct research on "green" and "fair trade" export markets and to provide information and training to local businesses. SMEs, in particular, should be supported and informed about the various fair trade and bio labels in the main Western markets and the conditions needed to obtain certification.

---

[125] So far, only one CDM project has taken place in El Salvador. It is a small landfill gas to energy project, which involves investors from Canada and the Netherlands together with the Government of Luxembourg. The CDM as it currently stands is due to be phased out in 2012, but it is likely to be renewed in the same or a similar form as part of the outcome of the Copenhagen conference.

b.   "Responsibility" measures

El Salvador has already initiated efforts to promote corporate social responsibility. EMPRESAL was established under the umbrella of FUNDEMAS. Following a diagnostic of the state of CSR in El Salvador in 2004, EMPRESAL has promoted the dissemination of good practices through workshops, direct advice and the preparation of practical guides. The programme is part of a regional network of institutions that promote CSR, including in Argentina, Brazil, Canada, Chile, Mexico and the United States. A number of foreign investors are currently involved in EMPRESAL through their membership in FUNDEMAS, including AES, Grupo Calvo, Microsoft and Wal-Mart.

In CAFTA-DR, the parties agree not to weaken labour protections in order to promote trade and investment. Labour standards are to be set nationally, but parties agree that national law and its enforcement will respect ILO conventions. El Salvador's labour code provides an appropriate balance between protecting workers' rights and the flexibilities needed by employers (chapter II).

El Salvador has achieved good labour standards but these are *de minimis* standards. Several zones already go beyond *de minimis* standards by providing on-site health clinics with doctors for zone workers and recreational facilities for workers and their families.[126] Health facilities are a public–private partnership, in the sense that clinic facilities are staffed and operated by the zone owners/operators while medicines and hospital treatment are state-provided.

These partnerships and CSR initiatives are in the public interest and in the enlightened self-interest of employers who value a healthy and productive workforce. They form an interesting basis on which to promote the zones to investors. There may be opportunities to enhance these partnerships in the following directions:

- Extend health facilities to workers' immediate families, especially children.

- Provide backup child-care support to working mothers.

- Initiate more opportunities for supplementary education and training for blue-collar workers in designated free periods granted by zone employers.

- A joint government/zone task force should develop a full list of enhancements and the respective roles of government, zone owners and employers. The Government could co-invest with private owners in high-standard facilities for workers.

- The work of EMPRESAL should be reinforced, including through increased participation in its work by the largest TNCs present in El Salvador.

c.   Principles of incentives for "green and responsible" investments

A number of incentives will probably be required in order to promote the development of above-average environmental and labour standards inside and outside of the zones. Such targeted incentives could substitute for the current generous tax incentives provided in EPZs, which are important in attracting investors but do not really give a competitive edge as their use – both regionally and globally – is so widespread (annex I).

---

[126] This applies, at least, to the two zones visited by the UNCTAD fact-finding mission. The clinics include full-time doctors, and appear to specialize in the health concerns of women, who make up the bulk of the zones' workforce.

The new range of incentives would create a distinctive profile for El Salvador and promote positive outcomes for workers and the environment. They should not lower tax revenue, as the exemption on corporate income tax for EPZ companies would be lifted to become WTO-compliant (chapter II). The incentives suggested below should be introduced in the context of bringing the zones within a uniform national corporate taxation regime. The recommendations assume that:

- The general taxation reforms proposed in Chapter II are adopted by 2015, in particular that: (a) corporate tax is applied to all enterprises, including zone companies; (b) faster tax depreciation is allowed for fixed assets; and (c) loss carry forward is permitted.

- Although zones will continue to be privately developed and owned, there is a strong public interest in assisting private owners to attract new investors and retain existing ones.

The recommended business incentives on investment in fixed assets are:

- "Green" and "responsible" fixed assets acquired from 2010 should be entitled to fast depreciation rates (up to 100 per cent) or tax credits, which are a highly favourable form of incentive that also actively promote the country's priority objectives and outcomes. In order to be effective, accelerated depreciation would have to be combined with the introduction of an indefinite loss carry-forward provision (chapter II and annex I).

- "Green" assets would be defined as those that lower energy use, emissions, waste or pollution by defined amounts or to meet best-in-class standards. They would comprise both common facilities established by zone owners (e.g. waste treatment, disposal and recycling) and clean production technologies implemented by zone producers (e.g. energy-saving equipment). "Responsible" assets would include employer-provided health, educational and child welfare facilities.

- Businesses should be able to defer the utilization of depreciation allowances and tax credits. Companies such as zone owners and producers that are currently exempt from corporate income tax could thus utilize these allowances and tax credits after 2015, or whenever they become subject to corporate income taxation.

- Businesses should be able to transfer allowances and tax credits to their subsidiaries in El Salvador so as to promote new investments.

- In the spirit of harmonization of taxation, these measures would apply generally, but the deferral and transfer provisions should be especially helpful to zone companies that are currently exempt from corporate income tax.

- Subject to a detailed calculation of revenue forgone, it might also be useful to apply a one-off provision for carry-back of unused depreciation allowances for a period of around 3–5 years (e.g. 2005 to 2009, or 2007 to 2009). This would assist businesses outside zones that have unutilized depreciation allowances due to the restrictions on loss carry-forward. For zone developers and producers, who have been tax-exempt, it would enable the full benefit of such allowances to be deployed once they became subject to corporate income taxes.

The recommended business incentives on operating costs for "green" and "responsible" activities are:

- Excess deduction of specified costs could be envisaged. These could include the expense of staff and consumables devoted to worker health, welfare and training activities, paid time off for worker training, and additional expenses arising from meeting top environmental standards.

- For tax-exempt enterprises (such as zone owners and enterprises), the ability to accumulate these specific deductions for deduction from taxable income when the tax exemptions expire should be considered.

In addition, El Salvador could consider putting in place a second bracket of lower corporate income tax for companies that operate entirely in "green" businesses, such as renewable energies, recycling technologies and others.

2. Tourism

The tourism sector has started to develop from an extremely low basis in the past few years, in large part as a result of the proactive efforts of the Ministry of Tourism established in 2004, PROESA, and other stakeholders in the sector. Nevertheless, El Salvador is still at a niche and underexploited stage of tourism development, and the sector underperforms its potential. In particular, the impact of tourism on sustainable development ("green" and "responsible") could be significantly increased, and FDI could make a contribution in that respect.

The number of overseas visitors steadily increased to 1.4 million in 2008 from 950,000 in 2004,[127] before declining in the first half of 2009 as a result of the global crisis. Business and family visits dominate, while leisure tourists represented less than 30 per cent of the total in 2008. In addition, 64 per cent of tourists came from lower-spending-power Central American countries and 30 per cent came from North America, a vast majority of whom were on family visits. By contrast, visitors from Europe represented less than 3 per cent in 2008. The total income from tourism reached $730 million in 2008, 3.3 per cent of GDP.

The contribution of leisure-based tourism to economic activity and development is thus still relatively limited and operating below its potential. As a comparison, the Dominican Republic attracted 4 million visitors in 2008, where tourism contributes to around 20 per cent of GDP. Costa Rica, which is perhaps closer to what El Salvador could offer than the Dominican Republic, attracted 2 million visitors in 2007, including almost 1 million from North America and 300,000 from Europe.

The Government is aware of the untapped potential. It prepared the first National Tourism Plan in 2006, which since then has been updated once. The headline goals of the plan are to increase the number of visitors to 3 million per annum by 2020 and the contribution of tourism to GDP to 10 per cent. In order to boost the industry's contribution to GDP, the plan proposes a greater focus on developed-country markets to boost arrivals and per-visitor spending. The meetings, incentives, conventions and exhibitions market is to be targeted to enhance the mix of visitors, although the potential of all market segments is considered. El Salvador's most prominent current niche is surf tourism, which is mostly catered for by small-scale beach lodgings.

The private investment strategy in the plan gives prominence to smaller hotels and hostels of up to 50 rooms, and to improving the capacity of restaurants and ancillary services to boost the economic impact of the industry. Private investment of $350 million to augment the number of rooms available is foreseen. This is a modest objective.

The National Tourism Plan is comprehensive and inclusive, and has the virtue of setting not only general objectives but also clear targets for industry development. It is helpful in detailing the actions needed by all stakeholders to achieve the targets. And yet, it would benefit from a number of additional FDI-related interventions:

---

[127] In addition to this, there was an increase in one-day excursions from abroad to almost 500,000 in 2008, from 80,000 in 2004.

● Large-scale tourism is at an incipient stage in El Salvador. There is an opportunity to generate benefits – and avoid mistakes – that have been identified in countries with more developed tourism industries. In particular, there is the opportunity to avoid outcomes in which large-scale resort-based tourism does not generate commensurate local benefits in the form of local supplies of goods and services because of its enclave nature. In that respect, the establishment of a linkages programme targeted at the tourism industry might be useful.

● At least one major investment each from leading North American and European developers/operators should be attracted. Flagship investments in the industry are important to put El Salvador on the map in these markets. This, of course, could be a co-investment with a local property investor. PROESA is working hard to attract such investors. The successful establishment and expansion of the Royal Decameron Salinitas resort (operated by Colombian interests) is an example, although of the all-inclusive type.

● Boutique and specialized foreign investors in the segments that offer most potential in El Salvador should be targeted, including high-end ecotourism, surfing, hiking and other outdoor activities. Ancillary services (guiding, transport, restaurants) are particularly important in these segments, and small specialized foreign investors can bring valuable expertise.

● If the "green and responsible" FDI strategy described above is adopted, there could be strong synergies with the development of tourism. Firstly, the suggested tax incentives would promote sustainable and environmentally friendly tourism. Secondly, there could be strong synergies in country marketing and branding.

● Leading hospitality training schools should be targeted to introduce the highest standards of client service by industry staff, and to teach and foster entrepreneurship by related service providers. The latter role is important, as local tourism-related services are so often microenterprises that may not be very appealing to tourists. The aim should be to build highly attractive local restaurants, events, attractions and services that will genuinely add to the appeal of visiting El Salvador. As an example, the Cornell-Nanyang Institute of Hospitality Management in Singapore aims to develop skills in entrepreneurship and innovation in the industry, and also to provide staff and management training.

3. Agriculture

Agriculture still represents around 14 per cent of GDP, and it employs about a quarter of the labour force, mostly the poorer segments of the population. Modernization of the sector is thus essential for sustainable development and poverty reduction. In particular, it is crucial that a larger share of small- and medium-scale farmers be enabled to operate on a sustainable commercial basis, and that they be prepared for the gradual phasing-out of tariff protection under CAFTA-DR.

As indicated in chapter II, El Salvador enforces a strict restriction on the size of agricultural land ownership by natural or legal persons.[128] The restriction imposes limitations on the development of large-scale farming, and restricts the type of FDI that El Salvador can attract in agricultural production. Given the sensitivity of rural land ownership issues, it is assumed that El Salvador will not wish at the moment to lift the size cap. This does not mean, however, that TNCs could not play a role in helping the sector to modernize and increase productivity, and in raising rural incomes.

---

[128] Ownership is limited to 245 hectares, except for farmers' cooperatives for which the restriction does not apply.

Contract farming (box III.2) offers an avenue through which foreign investors can support small- and medium-scale farmers, including through transfers of know-how and techniques, financing, extension services, increased stability and predictability (in terms of output and prices), and access to markets. Contract farming has become important around the world as a form of TNC involvement in agriculture (through equity participation or non-equity involvement). It exists in over 110 countries. In 2008, Nestlé worked with more than 600,000 contract farmers in 80 developing and transition economies. In turn, Unilever sourced agricultural inputs through contract farming with 100,000 farmers in developing countries in 2008. Many other large agro-industrial groups operate similarly.

Box III.2. Contract farming

Contract farming is an important form of TNC participation in agriculture in developing countries – distinct from traditional FDI where foreign investors directly acquire and run farms. It covers a variety of arrangements that involve different types of contractors, products, degrees of integration and numbers of stakeholders involved. Five basic types of contract farming arrangements can be distinguished:

- In the **centralized model**, a TNC sources its produce from a large number of farmers under a vertically coordinated arrangement. Quality is controlled by the TNC and quantities are determined at the beginning of the growing season. This model is used most frequently for produces that require a high degree of processing.

- The **nucleus estate model** is similar to the centralized model, except that the TNC also has its own production facilities to guarantee throughput. The nucleus farm can also be used as a "showcase" and experimental ground with capacity-building purposes for contract farmers.

- The **multipartite model** involves a joint venture between statutory entities and TNCs engaging with farmers.

- The **informal model** implies a looser relationship between farmers and TNCs. Contracts are more basic and typically on a seasonal basis. This model is typical for crops that require little processing.

- The **intermediary model** involves at least three different parties: An end-buyer (processor or major trader) formally contracts with an intermediary (collector or farmer's cooperative) who, in turn, contracts more or less formally with farmers. There is no direct link between the end-buyer and farmers in this model.

The TNCs involved in contract farming include mostly food processors, growers and wholesalers. Retail chains also engage in contract farming in a number of countries to source their supplies of fresh products. Both food and non-food agricultural products are subject to contract farming arrangements.

Sources: Eaton and Shepherd (2001) and UNCTAD (2009g).

Although there are many potential gains from integrating small- and medium-scale farmers in the commercial agro-business supply chain, including through contract farming with TNCs, there are also pitfalls that need to be avoided. In particular, it is essential to account for the "David and Goliath" nature of the relationship between small-scale farmers and TNCs. In order to promote the beneficial development of contract farming with TNCs in El Salvador, it is thus recommended to:[129]

---

[129] Eaton and Shepherd (2001) provide details on how to successfully foster and manage contract farming, including in terms of necessary pre-conditions and the specification of contracts.

- Consider the development of a regulatory framework for contract farming, as has been done in a number of countries recently.[130] The framework should cover the rights and obligations of each party.

- Consider the preparation of model contracts, as part of government-led efforts to educate and train farmers in cooperating with TNCs. Several models of contract could be prepared to account for varying degrees of commitment and coordination between parties. The issues covered would include – among others – the duration of the contract, quality standards, quantities, cultivation practices, delivery, prices and insurance.

- Mandate the Superintendence of Competition to monitor contract farming practices if and when they develop, in particular to avoid abuses of dominant position.

- Commission PROESA to promote contract farming as part of its efforts to attract foreign investors in agro-industry.

D. Implications for investment promotion and PROESA

The strategy of using FDI in support of national competitiveness and in promoting sustainable development has a number of implications for El Salvador's investment promotion efforts. PROESA is on the front line, and it may have to make some adjustments in its work and investment targets. It is also suggested below that PROESA take on a number of additional tasks, including in terms of aftercare, advocacy and outreach to the diaspora. This would require additional human and financial resources for the agency.

The increase in resources is not quantified, as a detailed review of PROESA's structure and needs was not part of the mandate of this review. Existing vacancies, however, should be filled as a starting point and as a matter of priority. Other institutions would also be involved in implementing the strategy proposed above, and there are implications for the nation as a whole, mostly in terms of image-building.

I. Image-building

El Salvador has a low profile among foreign investors, particularly outside the Americas, and it continues to suffer from the images of the civil war. PROESA, however, has worked hard to improve the country's image and generate site visits by targeted investors. The Ministry of Tourism has engaged resources in promoting the image of the country to tourists. In the vast majority of cases, first-time visitors are surprised and impressed by the conditions they find upon arrival. Clearly, there is a large gap between reality and image.

As a result, the conditions are ripe for El Salvador to invest more significant resources in image-building, in addition to the efforts to generate targeted site visits. Such image-building campaigns tend to be expensive, but are very productive when new visitors are almost guaranteed to be pleasantly surprised. If the strategy to promote "green and responsible investments" is adopted, it could provide a unique image and branding tool, as well as being one way to target the audience. The focus would not only allow El Salvador to "brand" itself, but would also benefit locally established businesses wishing to tap the "green and responsible" market and firm up their CSR credentials. It would also be an opportunity to change the image of "maquilas" and abandon the term. The word has a rather negative connotation and does not fit with what El Salvador wishes its zones to be.

---

[130] India, Thailand and Viet Nam, for example, introduced regulations on contract farming in the past decade.

An image-building campaign on investment should be coordinated with the efforts undertaken by the Ministry of Tourism. Although the target audiences are very different, there can be strong synergies. It is indeed important for the investment-oriented image-building campaign to just put El Salvador on the radar screen in certain countries, and tourism promotion can help in that respect. In addition, El Salvador could jointly promote itself as a "green" destination for tourism as well as a "green" destination for investment.

El Salvador is by and large an unknown quantity in Asia among the investor community, notwithstanding the opportunities offered under CAFTA-DR. China, India, Japan, the Republic of Korea and Taiwan Province of China are the important targets for El Salvador to attract Asian investors to produce for the United States market. However, since it is difficult and expensive for a small country to make an impact in large far-off Asian locations, it may be more cost-effective for El Salvador to propose to CACM members a regional marketing campaign in Asia. This should promote the Central American region as a gateway to the United States market, as well as profiling its regional market. This would set the tone for follow-up direct marketing and site visits in which El Salvador can justifiably present itself as a leading regional candidate for FDI. A regional campaign might attract United States funding as part of efforts to deliver developmental benefits from CAFTA-DR.

European TNCs have a modest presence, including, surprisingly, TNCs from Spain. Spanish investment has been prominent in banking, telecommunications, tourism and electricity, for example in Central and South America. The Economic Partnership Agreement with the European Union, upon completion, should be exploited for opportunities to raise the image both of the region and of El Salvador.

In North America, the presence of a diaspora of 2 million people gives El Salvador a good starting point, and a more direct "mass" approach to investors is possible (section 2). The most likely source of direct interest is United States companies, since they have headquarters and investment strategy decision-making based in the United States. Nevertheless, non–United States companies may often have regional headquarters in the United States, and these can form a useful starting point for marketing approaches.

2.   Outreach to the diaspora

Many countries have policies to encourage inward investment from their diaspora, who seem an obvious source of capital and skills. Usually, the overall results are disappointing in generating investment from members of the diaspora themselves. PROESA could try a different approach, learning from the experience of Cathedral Art, a United States–based company that invested in El Salvador to produce religious ornaments and jewellery. The company's interest in El Salvador was sparked by the high quality of its Salvadorean workforce in the United States.

A marketing initiative could be developed to spur the diaspora workforce in United States companies to become an overseas "sales force" for PROESA to generate interest in site visits. In the past, Ireland did something similar by successfully targeting United States corporations whose CEOs had Irish names. This approach would supplement, not replace, the current highly targeted sales approach of PROESA. It would enable the net to be cast wide and not begin with pre-conceived ideas regarding which industries might be attracted to invest in El Salvador. As indicated above, sectoral targeting has limitations, and no IPA anywhere, for example, would have thought of religious products as a potential FDI target.

Since around 2 million Salvadoreans live in the United States, there are likely to be several hundred thousand actively employed in United States companies at all levels of responsibility. How could this formidable sales force be mobilized to generate investor interest in El Salvador leading to information-seeking and site visits? PROESA could take the lead to:

- Develop brief brochures on the opportunities and benefits of investing in El Salvador. These could be generic to any industry. They should be suitable for handing over to executives of United States companies and should include contact numbers of the PROESA sales team.

- Create a desk at the San Salvador airport departures area to promote the programme to Salvadoreans returning to the United States from holiday. A database of willing participants and their employers should be developed on that basis.

- Set up a two-step prize system for investor responses initiated by the programme. A small prize could be awarded for enquiries generated by the system that led to a site visit. A second larger prize could be awarded for a completed investment that originates from the programme.

- Publicize successful cases of investments to motivate others.

- Include all Salvadorean workers in the United States, whether they are blue-collar or white-collar.

3. PROESA's sectoral targets

PROESA is a relatively small investment promotion agency (IPA) in relation to El Salvador's size and level of economic activity, and in comparison with investment promotion agencies elsewhere. It concentrates on investor attraction through proactive targeting, and devotes relatively few resources to facilitation and advocacy. It is notable among IPAs familiar to the UNCTAD review team for the directness and clarity of its sales objectives. A number of pioneering foreign investments have been attracted in significant part as a result of its efforts (chapter I).

PROESA currently operates on the basis of nine key sectoral targets. Given the small size of the organization and limited resources, it is important for PROESA to keep reviewing these targets and to be willing to adjust them as needed in view of results, impacts and national strategic priorities. In order to leverage FDI in support of national competitiveness, PROESA should add two key priorities to its targeting list:

- **FDI in higher education:** PROESA should target FDI into university, technical education and foreign language training. The targets should be identified in consultation with the Ministry of Education and other relevant stakeholders.

- **FDI in infrastructure:** Investment in transport should be the priority. PROESA's valuable experience in targeting and dealing with foreign investors should be fully used to secure a reputable international ports operator for La Unión. It should thus be involved in a process led by the Comisión Ejecutiva Portuaria Autónoma (CEPAL). It should also promote co-investment by local and foreign partners in road concessions, starting in San Salvador. The long-term aim of road concessioning should be to build the capability of the local construction industry and related technical and professional service providers to invest in PPPs in the region.

In addition, if the "green and responsible" strategy is to be adopted, PROESA could focus some of its targeting efforts on TNCs involved in the production of bio and "green" products, in clean and/or low-carbon production processes and those actively promoting their CSR focus. The companies that signed up to the Global Compact offer a good starting point.

4.   Aftercare and policy advocacy

PROESA's work on aftercare and policy advocacy is relatively limited, as the agency is focused on generating country visits by prospective investors. There is strong international evidence, however, that aftercare is a useful tool to promote reinvestments and to enhance the positive impacts of TNC activities through linkages, increased local value-addition and upward movement along the value chain. UNCTAD (2007) elaborates on the benefits of aftercare and the types of efforts that can be undertaken. These revolve around administrative, operational and strategic services. To a large extent, aftercare should be considered as the continuation of successful targeting activities.

Given that El Salvador's investment climate is generally favourable to FDI (chapter II), the need for advocacy is more moderate than in countries with bigger weaknesses in their investment framework. Nevertheless, the FDI attraction strategies proposed above would require careful preparatory work involving the Government and the private sector before they could lead to a targeting campaign by PROESA. Two issues would have to be addressed:

- Parts of the regulatory framework would have to be adapted (e.g. education, corporate taxation, financial markets);

- FDI would best benefit El Salvador if local partners are fully prepared to be involved (e.g. in terms of linkages or road concessioning).

PROESA cannot act alone on these matters, but it should take an active advocacy role in ensuring that reforms are undertaken and that the groundwork is done well, so as to attract FDI and derive the most benefit from it. The precise amount of resources dedicated to advocacy by PROESA needs to be determined, but the efforts should involve senior management as well as the National Commission for Export and Investment Promotion (Comisión Nacional de Promoción de Exportaciones e Inversiones (CONADEI)). The work should be structured along the "policy advocacy cycle" in four main stages:[131]

- Identifying "problems" and setting the agenda;

- Developing the most effective policy remedy;

- Advocating the policy; and

- Monitoring progress and evaluating results/impacts.

5.   Synergies in investment and export promotion

Investment and export promotion efforts are both under the overall supervision of CONADEI. Until recently, the two functions were carried out independently by PROESA and EXPORTA. The two agencies reported to CONADEI but operated with a separate management structure and a large degree of autonomy. Until recently, also, CONADEI was chaired by the Vice-President. In July 2009, the newly elected Government placed CONADEI under the authority of the Minister of Economy. In late 2009, it was also decided to put PROESA and EXPORTA under a single management structure and to build stronger synergies between investment and export promotion functions.

Institutional arrangements on investment and export promotion vary around the world. A report by UNCTAD shows that 42 per cent of IPAs double as export promotion agencies.[132] Combined agencies

---

[131] UNCTAD (2008) provides a detailed discussion of the work of investment promotion agencies as policy advocates. It describes the policy advocacy cycle in greater detail and gives concrete recommendations on how best to structure such efforts.

[132] UNCTAD (2009c). The study reviews practices among 173 IPAs on all continents, including developing and developed countries. It provides a comprehensive analysis of the pros and cons of both institutional arrangements.

tend to be more frequent in small economies, probably as a way to rationalize the use of scarce resources and to better combine international marketing efforts. No clear-cut solution can be advocated under all circumstances on the institutional arrangement, as there are pros and cons to either arrangement.

The advantages of combining the two functions include: (a) better policy coherence in investment and trade issues; (b) shared infrastructure and administrative services; (c) knowledge-sharing; (d) potential synergies in overseas promotion and image-building; and (e) common ground for policy advocacy. The disadvantages include: (a) possible loss of focus, as objectives and core activities differ widely; (b) different time frames; (c) different clients and contact points in companies; (d) different skill requirements from the staff; and (e) possible loss of focus on investment promotion and investment-related advocacy.

The disadvantages highlighted above indicate that whatever the institutional arrangement chosen, it is important to preserve some independence between the two functions. In a country such as El Salvador, which has made a firm choice to develop as an open economy, however, it is important that synergies between investment and export promotion be maximized. A large proportion of foreign investors attracted to El Salvador will indeed be interested in the country as an export platform.

The process of bringing PROESA and EXPORTA under a single management structure is still a work in progress. As the process unfolds, it will be important to nurture the respective competences and focus of the two functions, while also maximizing the new opportunities for synergies and cooperation between staff members. The possibilities for synergies include more extensive use of EXPORTA's existing literature on export potential when promoting El Salvador as a base for export-oriented investments; ensuring that prospective investors are introduced to colleagues in charge of export promotion; and efforts to internationalize local companies, from tapping export markets to working as local suppliers for TNCs. The new agency will probably also need to define a new image and name to communicate with investors and exporters.

6.   Infrastructure concessions

A highly skilled unit is needed within the Government to structure infrastructure transactions, working with the sector ministries involved. Such a unit has not been established in El Salvador, and the conduct of the concessioning of La Unión indicates that specialized expertise is urgently required. Although IPAs sometimes undertake this role (as Proinversión in Peru does), it would probably create an excessive burden on PROESA to do so. A dedicated unit would probably be better established under the supervision of the Ministry of Public Works. PROESA could nevertheless still provide valuable contributions to the work of the unit through close cooperation on issues relating to foreign investors.

IV. MAIN CONCLUSIONS AND RECOMMENDATIONS

El Salvador made a carefully considered and resolute strategic choice to pursue socio-economic development under an open and regulated market economy setting, decades ago. As a small country, it was the appropriate decision, and it remains the best option for El Salvador to achieve its development goals. It has also been the strategic choice of all successful small countries around the world.

El Salvador has done well on several fronts, including in terms of the regulatory framework for investment, the use of e-governance, the development of key backbone infrastructure, and policy coherence. In addition, the smooth political transition of June 2009 was a clear demonstration of the strength of El Salvador's democracy, and it further solidified socio-political stability.

The country has legitimate aspirations to significantly raise the standards of living of the population, and the Government is intent on making a sharp dent in poverty and inequality. In order to achieve these goals, El Salvador needs to rise to the high end of the group of upper middle-income countries, i.e. raise per capita gross national income from below $3,500 to around $10,000. This is a formidable challenge that few non-oil economies have achieved or surpassed, but it is within El Salvador's ability.

A number of intermediate steps and policies to address key weaknesses will be needed in order to achieve the long-term development goals. In the context of El Salvador's small open economy, FDI could make a significant contribution, both in terms of the intermediate steps and in terms of the long-term objective. Two key catalytic and positive effects of FDI should be proactively pursued and promoted through a mix of regulatory, policy and investment promotion measures:

- FDI in support of national competitiveness; and
- FDI for sustainable development.

Concrete measures to promote these catalytic effects are proposed below.

A. FDI in support of national competitiveness

A competitive business climate is essential to the development of a small, open economy such as El Salvador as it seeks to produce goods and services for the region and for the major OECD markets. Two key components influence the ability of national companies to reach international levels of competitiveness[133] and the capacity of the country to attract foreign investors in search of regional or worldwide production sites that are part of global value chains: (a) the quality of the investment framework; and (b) the availability of high-quality and reliable physical infrastructure and human capital at reasonable costs. The Government of El Salvador is in a position to influence both components with appropriate policies.

I. Achieve global excellence in investment-related regulation and facilitation

As a small economy, El Salvador should seek to enhance its appeal to foreign investors by establishing a highly efficient and effective regulatory system. Such a system ought to facilitate and promote investment, and protect the national interest. Two key aspects are concerned:

- The quality and adequacy of laws and regulations; and
- The quality and effectiveness of implementation and administration of rules.

---

[133] This encompasses the capacity to export globally and internationalize operations, including through outward FDI.

This review recommends actions in priority areas, either in terms of legal changes or in terms of administration.

a. Review corporate taxation

Although most aspects of the current corporate tax regime are sound, some crucial weaknesses and challenges remain, including the compatibility of the EPZ regime with WTO regulations, the low level of tax revenue, the overall structure of investment incentives, and the administrative burden. It will be important for El Salvador to resist calls to replace all tax breaks; it will be important to avoid a proliferation of sector-specific incentives. The costs and benefits of incentives are more difficult to assess as they multiply, and it is also increasingly difficult to resist calls for special treatment by one sector when other sectors benefit from specific tax breaks. In order not to fall onto a slippery slope of a proliferation of incentives, it may be worthwhile considering a regime that offers a level playing field, with targeted incentives contingent upon general outcomes such as job creation, training or expansion.

Concretely, it is recommended to:

- Unify the tax system by integrating the EPZ regime into a reformed general regime compatible with WTO regulations;

- Carefully analyse the cost/benefit ratio of incentives provided under the Law on International Services and keep the option open of integrating eligible services into the general regime, particularly if more targeted incentives are put in place;

- Compensate the phasing out of export-dependent incentives and introduce pro-investment measures by: (a) reviewing the headline corporate income tax rate in light of the options considered for incentives; (b) allowing faster depreciation of assets; (c) introducing an indefinite loss carry-forward provision; and (d) replacing the monthly advance payments on corporate income taxes with a quarterly or semi-annual system based on self-assessment rather than turnover;

- Introduce limited and targeted incentives to promote specific outcomes. These would be linked in particular to the promotion of "responsible" and "green" investments that could bring particular benefits to El Salvador in terms of job creation and sustainable investments (see below);

- Introduce two new VAT rates to increase revenue while sheltering the poor: one low rate for essential goods and services and one high rate for non-essential or luxury goods and services;

- Negotiate and ratify DTTs with the main existing and potential source countries of FDI.

b. Bring the customs office to global standards of excellence

Much progress has been achieved in improving the customs service, both in its facilitation and in its control functions. Given its open economy model of development and the export orientation of most of its foreign investors, however, El Salvador needs to bring the customs office to global standards of excellence, with a particular emphasis on trade facilitation. The following is recommended:

- Benchmark trade facilitation services against the world's most efficient and diligent customs administrations in the world, which include Denmark, Hong Kong (China) and Singapore.

- Increase the use of e-tools in customs administration.

- Give high priority to the migration from ASYCUDA++ to ASYCUDA World.

- Adjust the vision, mission and objectives statements of the customs administration to promote a stronger mentality shift towards trade facilitation.

c. Support the work of the Superintendence of Competition

The adoption of the competition law and the creation of the Superintendence of Competition are recent milestones for El Salvador, which should help it to maximize the benefits of the presence of foreign investors. The legal framework is of a high standard, and the Superintendence has firmly established its competence and credibility in a short period of time. The effectiveness of the competition regime, however, is hampered by the difficulty of enforcing the rulings of the Superintendence and by the slow appeals process.

It is essential that appeals procedures be accelerated and that cases currently with the Supreme Court be brought to ruling. At the same time, judges sitting on the administrative chamber of the Supreme Court should receive appropriate training on competition issues, perhaps with the support of academia and international organizations.

In addition, the advocacy work of the Superintendence should be strengthened further. In order to ensure that competition issues are appropriately reflected across all key government policies, it would also be useful for El Salvador to adopt a formal competition policy.

d. Improve or clarify certain provisions specific to foreign investors

El Salvador offers an open, favourable, non-discriminatory and protective regime to foreign investors. While no major changes are called for on FDI-specific legislation, some clarifications or adaptations could bring additional credibility and promote foreign investment:

- The protection offered to small local businesses from FDI should be clarified and better defined by law.

- Registration with the ONI has proved ineffective and has been incompletely applied. Compulsory registration of foreign investors could be removed, and the facilitation services offered by the ONI could be integrated into the CNR, which would become the single point of entry for all investors setting up their business – national as well as foreign.

- It would be useful for El Salvador to negotiate additional bilateral investment treaties with countries that are emerging or could emerge as key sources of FDI. Targets should include Brazil, China, Colombia, India and Singapore.

e. Ensure an effective implementation and administration of laws and regulations

El Salvador has performed relatively well in establishing the institutions in charge of implementing and administering the regulatory framework for investment. The strength and competence of the Superintendence of Competition and SIGET are particularly noteworthy. In addition, it has performed well in using e-tools in public administration (e.g. at the CNR) and in reducing the burden of administrative procedures.

Efforts towards the effective and efficient enforcement of rules and regulation need to be continued, however. In particular, it is recommended to:

- Continue to identify regulations whose administrative burden could be reduced or those that may be redundant or unnecessary, as was previously done under the El Salvador Eficiente programme.

- Continue the implementation and extension of the e-regulations programme with UNCTAD's technical assistance. This should facilitate access to information and ease establishment and operational procedures for foreign investors as well national companies, including SMEs.

- Further invest in the capacity of key regulatory institutions, in particular the tax administration, the Superintendence of Competition, and SIGET.

- Work to instil a culture of service across all administrations that are directly or indirectly in contact with investors. Achieving global excellence in the general framework for investment requires that regulators understand that their role is not exclusively to control and enforce, but also to service and facilitate investment within a well-defined set of rules. A number of countries have established "client charters" specifying the level of service that investors may expect from the administration to achieve this purpose. This option could be considered in El Salvador, and PROESA could play a role in sensitizing and training civil servants on the needs and perspectives of investors.

2. Leverage FDI for skills development, and excel in building and training human capital

The labour force is one of El Salvador's greatest assets in attracting FDI. While Salvadorean workers are widely regarded as productive and very receptive to training, the general level of education remains unsatisfactory. The country continues to suffer from skills shortages in a wide range of occupations, and the insufficient knowledge of English is widely considered as a key handicap.

In order to compete in attracting foreign investors, move up the value chain and increase productivity and wages, it is essential that El Salvador excel in building and training human capital. Increased public investment in education is required, and two sets of recommendations linked to foreign investment can be offered. Firstly, the country ought to put in place a proactive policy to attract FDI in higher education and vocational training, in order to bring about higher quality in the universities and technical schools. Secondly, El Salvador ought to revamp its regulations on the employment of foreigners, in order to make it easier for investors to rely on expatriates when local skills are in short supply or unavailable.

a. Promote FDI in higher education

Although the presence of skilled expatriates may bring benefits to the country and fill temporary gaps, El Salvador must, first and foremost, build the capacity of its own population. The higher education system is currently extremely fragmented and not always up to the desired quality standards. In the national interest and that of its students, El Salvador ought to enforce stricter quality controls on its universities and expose institutions of higher learning to international practices. It also ought to proactively attempt to attract foreign investment in higher education as a tool to diversify the offer, raise quality standards, and potentially become an education services hub in the region.

Regulatory measures

- Remove potential regulatory barriers to FDI. In particular, the requirement for new institutions of higher learning to offer programmes in at least 5 different fields and the requirement that new universities correspond to an "objective need of the country" may prevent internationally recognized universities from establishing specialized schools in El Salvador, even though they may be of great benefit to the country.

- Strengthen quality controls on universities by making the accreditation process compulsory.

- Establish a category of intermediate schools and degrees for centres that cannot obtain full accreditation but still meet quality requirements. This could be similar to the community or junior colleges in the United States that offer two-year programmes and grant associate degrees of legal assistant, technician or IT specialist.

Policy and institutional measures

- Join the European-led Bologna Process under the Bologna Policy Forum to expose universities to international standards and practices and ultimately promote the exchange of students, researchers and professors.

- Promote region-wide recognition of qualifications and the development of an education hub by taking the lead towards the creation of a Central American Higher Education Area, set up along the lines of the Bologna Process.

- Consider the potential role of for-profit institutions in selected fields.

- Build bridges between universities and the private sector, including in defining curricula, in promoting internships and visiting professorships, and by establishing an incubator fund to promote R&D-based joint ventures between universities and the private sector.

- Make FDI attraction in higher education an additional targeting priority for PROESA.

b.   Facilitate the temporary entry of expatriates with skills in short supply

El Salvador implements an outdated system of allocation of work permits for foreigners, and it has a very small expatriate workforce despite prevailing skills shortages. A new approach is recommended that would facilitate the entry of expatriates on a temporary basis, inasmuch as they possess skills that are in short supply. The new system would work along similar lines to the HI-B visas system in the United States. Skills in short supply would have to be identified and defined, and a national quota of visas would be determined on an annual basis. Work permits would be linked to the employer and issued for a period of up to three years, under a simplified administrative procedure.

3.   Strengthen infrastructure through FDI

El Salvador has developed reasonably good infrastructure services, in part as a result of investments by foreign investors. The roads network is particularly well developed for a country at this level of development, and the telecommunication, electricity and airport infrastructure are good too. The biggest shortfall concerns port infrastructure. The port of La Unión is so far not operational, which is a key weakness for the country.

Given its export orientation and the need to attract investors that are part of global value chains, it is vital for El Salvador to become or remain competitive, either regionally or globally, in providing key infrastructure services to investors. As the country has already experienced, it is possible to attract foreign investors to develop key parts of the nation's infrastructure, if an appropriate regulatory framework is in place. In order to further attract such investors, it is recommended to:

- Rapidly make La Unión operational by concluding a concession agreement with a leading and internationally recognized port operator capable of turning the port into a regional hub. Expert advice from investment banking and technical advisers should be sought, amongst other things to define appropriate commercial terms and conditions;

- Adopt a legal framework for private–public partnership agreements in infrastructure projects;

- Prepare an indicative electricity Master Plan providing medium- and long-term demand forecasts and highlighting the areas where investment in generation, transmission and distribution are most needed. The Master Plan should also help El Salvador promote the energy mix that it wishes to achieve and should attract private investors; and

- Investigate the possibility of concessioning the development of parts of the road network, particularly in the San Salvador area.

4. Establish a thriving capital market

Putting in place a thriving and efficient capital market should be considered as a top strategic priority for El Salvador. Efficient financial intermediation is essential not only for the development of local enterprises and their internationalization, but also for the attraction of foreign investors, in particular in infrastructure. A number of measures should be considered, including:

- Establishing a national task force to coordinate the preparation of a capital markets development policy for submission to Cabinet by the end of 2010. The experience of Chile in building an efficient capital market should be carefully analysed;

- Simplifying and clarify stock listing requirements;

- Putting in place a legal framework for mutual funds and venture capital funds;

- Granting more flexibility in investment decision to pension funds, under strict regulatory oversight; and

- Establishing a dialogue on corporate lending policies and practices with the banking industry.

5. Foster linkages and internationalize local companies

The availability of a competitive network of local suppliers is an important element of a country's attractiveness to foreign investors. In addition, sustained contractual links between national companies (including SMEs) and locally established TNCs are one of the major channels through which the economy as a whole can benefit from FDI. Such linkages facilitate the diffusion of information, technology, skills and management practices. They are also likely to reinforce the ability of suppliers to become exporters, and eventually to internationalize through outward FDI.

Setting up a proactive linkages programme should thus aim to achieve the twin benefits of improving the attractiveness of El Salvador as a destination for investment, and improving productivity in national enterprises. El Salvador could consider:

- Establishing an information database of linkages opportunities for TNCs and suppliers;

- Promoting direct training and skills transfers from TNCs to their suppliers, in addition to providing government-sponsored support to suppliers. This may include limited tax incentives to the benefit of companies providing training and skills transfers;

- Implementing UNCTAD's linkages programmes (which have been successfully established in other countries); and

● Putting in place a holistic approach to linkages and supplier development programmes, by targeting TNCs that have a well-developed philosophy and capacity to implement them in host countries.

B. FDI for sustainable development

El Salvador's environment is relatively fragile and under stress. The Law on Environment was adopted in 1998 in recognition of this and in an effort to protect the country from unsustainable exploitation of natural resources and deterioration of the environment. While the implementation of the law led to some harmful administrative bottlenecks in authorizations for investments, the situation has much improved since 2006, and El Salvador currently has a mostly appropriate regulatory system in place.

At the same time, international concerns about sustainable development – including as a result of climate change – have increased rapidly. Efforts are being stepped up worldwide to adapt modes of production to rising energy prices and the need/commitments to reduce greenhouse gas emissions, in particular in the context of the UNFCCC-driven Kyoto Protocol and the Copenhagen conference. TNCs around the world are taking note of these developments and are planning future strategies of adaptation to new regulations and standards.

Even before the strong emergence of environmental concerns on the international stage, many TNCs around the world had started to pay increasing attention to labour and corporate social responsibility issues. Although most reacted to pressure from consumers and advocacy groups in OECD countries – as opposed to producing self-generated decisions, the impacts on strategies are nonetheless real. In 2000, the United Nations launched the Global Compact as a policy platform and a practical framework to promote sustainable and responsible business practices. By late 2009, more than 5,200 corporations had signed up to the Global Compact, including almost 170 TNCs from the Financial Times 500 list of the world's largest companies.

El Salvador could take these global developments as constraints to its development. Alternatively, it could turn them into an opportunity to promote its own sustainable development and generate a clear and distinctive profile for FDI attraction. It is proposed that El Salvador should put in place policies and incentives to promote "green and responsible" FDI.

These policies could be tested in the EPZs at first, as part of measures implemented to adapt to the scheduled elimination of most tax incentives as they currently stand, in order to become compliant with WTO rules by 2015. Ensuring the durability of EPZ investments will indeed require that a new business rationale be developed. Close proximity to the United States market is one strong reason, which could be complemented by an appealing "green and responsible" EPZ profile for TNCs sensitive to these issues. If successful, the "green and responsible" strategy ought to be extended to the nation as a whole.

To promote "green and responsible" sustainable investment, El Salvador could:

● Prepare a policy and strategy of environmentally sustainable development to guide and underpin government policies, programmes and plans in a wide range of areas, including industry, infrastructure development, agriculture, tourism and urban planning;

● Strengthen the environmental strategy evaluations mechanism, including as an institutional tool to make the overall sustainability policy effective;

● Participate fully and constructively in the environmental initiatives of CAFTA-DR and in the post-Copenhagen process;

- Promote or require the use of carbon accounting under an internationally accepted methodology;

- Complete the set of technical norms and regulations to facilitate the preparation and evaluation of EIAs;

- Promote the development of renewable electricity sources through the proposed Electricity Master Plan;

- Increase the use of the Clean Development Mechanism set up as part of the Kyoto Protocol;

- Further improve labour and health standards both inside and outside EPZs, including in partnership with zone developers and companies;

- Introduce tax incentives for "green" and "responsible" investments in fixed assets, such as tax credits or accelerated depreciation, combined with an indefinite loss carry-forward provision;

- Introduce tax breaks on "green" and "responsible" operating costs;

- Consider the introduction of a second bracket of lower corporate income tax rate for companies that operate entirely in "green" businesses, such as renewable energies, recycling and others.

C. Implications for investment promotion and PROESA

The strategy of using FDI in support of national competitiveness and in promoting sustainable development has a number of implications for El Salvador's investment promotion efforts. PROESA/ CONADEI would have to play a key role, and would need to secure additional resources in order to taken on the new tasks suggested below. Other institutions would be affected as well. The largest implications touch upon six main issues:

- **Image-building:** El Salvador continues to suffer from an image deficit and a low international profile. With reality on the ground far better than common perceptions, the conditions are ripe for El Salvador to invest more significant resources in image-building. Such a campaign could build on the "green and responsible investment" strategy if it is adopted, and should be coordinated with efforts from the Ministry of Tourism. Coordinated efforts with CACM partners should also be considered to raise the profile of the region as a whole in Europe and Asia.

- **Outreach to the diaspora:** The Government should encourage overseas Salvadoreans to act as a "sales force" for PROESA and to generate interest in site visits. This could be done by preparing special brochures on business opportunities and on the benefits of investing in El Salvador; by setting up a desk at the airport in San Salvador to "recruit" agents; or by providing a two-step prize system for investor responses generated by the programme (for site visits and for completed investments).

- **PROESA's sectoral targets:** Sectoral targets should be reviewed if and when needed, to stay in line with strategic priorities and investment potential. Two new sectoral targets should be added at this juncture: FDI in higher education and FDI in infrastructure. TNCs with a focus on "green" products or production methods and those with a good track record on CSR should also be targeted.

- **Aftercare and policy advocacy:** If the strategies and policies proposed above are to be implemented, it will be important for PROESA to take the lead in advocating reforms related to

FDI. A strengthening of aftercare services could also lead to bigger reinvestments, more significant linkages and higher local value-addition.

- **Synergies in investment and trade promotion:** PROESA and EXPORTA operated until recently as separate organizations reporting to CONADEI; the former promoting FDI and the latter supporting exports. It was decided in late 2009 to bring the two institutions under a single management structure. As the merging process unfolds, it will be important to maximize synergies between the two functions, while also avoiding a dilution of the focus and respective skills and competences.

- **Infrastructure concessions:** It would be useful to set up a highly skilled and specialized unit within the Government to prepare and lead infrastructure concessions.

ANNEX I: INTERNATIONAL TAX COMPARISON

The burden of corporate taxes – evaluated as the total of the taxes collected by the Government over the 10 years as a percentage of the project cash flow (annex II) – is relatively moderate in El Salvador. For most sectors under consideration, the present value of taxes as a percentage of the project cash flow (PV tax) is either at a par with or below the level of neighbouring countries or other global comparators.

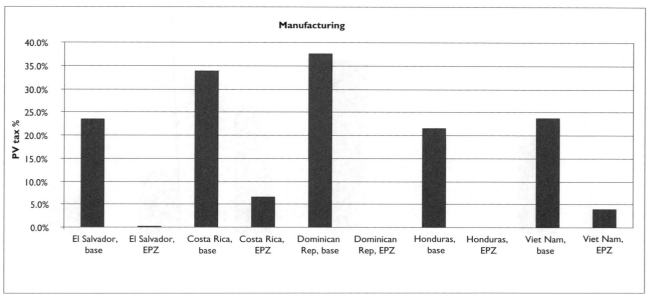

Source: UNCTAD.

Similarly to most countries in the region and beyond which operate export processing zones, El Salvador offers a virtually tax-free environment for export-oriented companies (table A.I.1). In addition to the merchandise exports regime, however, El Salvador also offers extremely generous incentives to exporters of services under the Law on International Services of 2007. As for EPZ companies, exporters of a range of services may benefit from a virtually tax-free environment.

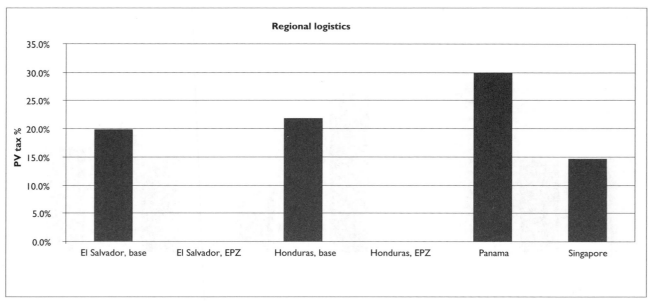

Source: UNCTAD.

Bringing tax incentives into compliance with WTO obligations will require that El Salvador eliminate tax breaks conditioned upon export performance by 2015, at least as far as merchandise exports are concerned. As recommended in chapter II, it is suggested that El Salvador bring the entire export-oriented regime (merchandise and services) into the general tax regime. This would widen the tax base and eliminate excessively generous tax incentives, as there is little justification for entire sectors to be fully exempt of corporate taxation.

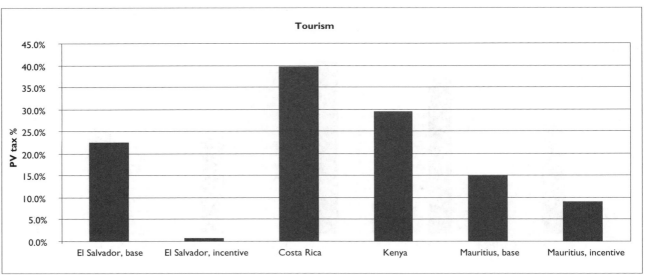

Source: UNCTAD.

It is understandable, however, that El Salvador should be concerned about the impact of the elimination of such incentives on investment – existing or potential. Consequently, this review suggests that improvements be introduced in the general regime at the same time as export-based incentives are phased out. Such improvements aim to promote investment in general, and are very widely applied around the world. In particular, the introduction of a loss carry-forward provision and accelerated depreciation would be very potent instruments to promote investment. In addition, this review suggests that targeted incentives could be introduced to promote national development goals, including the promotion of "green and responsible" investments. Such incentives could also be used to avoid the possible adverse effects on investment of phasing out export-oriented incentives.

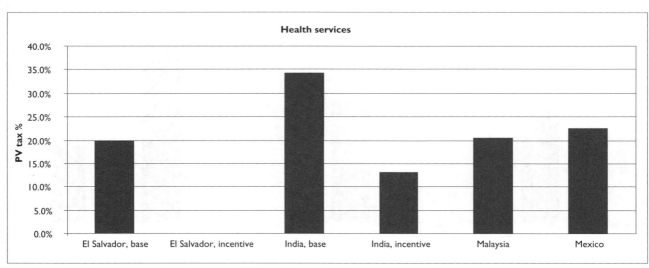

Source: UNCTAD.

Table A.I.I. Overview of tax structures in Central American countries

	El Salvador	Costa Rica	Guatemala	Honduras	Panama
Corporate income tax rate	25%	30%	31% or 5% of turnover	25%	30%
Loss carry-forward	none	3 years (industry) 5 years (agriculture)	5 years (capital losses) None (operational losses)	3 years (agriculture, manufacturing, mining, tourism)	5 years
Dividend withholding tax rate	0%	15%	0%	0%	10–20%
Tax depreciation:					
Method	straight-line	straight-line	straight-line	straight-line	straight-line
Standard rates	Buildings: 5% Machinery: 20% Vehicles: 25% Software: 25%	Buildings: 2–6% Machinery: 7–15% Vehicles: 10%	Buildings: 5% Machinery: 20% Vehicles: 20% Software: 33%		Buildings: up to 33% Machinery: up to 33% Vehicles: up to 33%
EPZ/maquila regime:	yes	yes	yes	yes	yes
Corporate income tax rate	0%	0%	0%	0%	0%
Local tax exemption	yes	yes	yes	yes	yes
Indirect tax exemption (import duties, VAT …)	yes	yes	yes	yes	yes
Dividend withholding tax rate	0%	15%	0%	0%	10%
Sectors benefiting from incentives	International distribution and logistics Call centres IT services R&D Aircraft and boat maintenance BPO Medical services Int'l financial services Tourism	Small businesses Hotels Air transportation Maritime transportation Car rental	Services sectors are eligible to EPZ incentives	Tourism Electricity generation from renewable sources	Tourism Forestry

Sources: National legislation and PricewaterhouseCoopers worldwide tax summaries.

ANNEX II: METHODOLOGY OF INTERNATIONAL TAX COMPARISONS

The Comparative Taxation Survey compares taxation on investment in several sectors in El Salvador with taxation in other selected countries – neighbours and countries elsewhere that have succeeded in attracting FDI to the sectors concerned. These comparisons enable El Salvador to assess the competitiveness of its taxation.

Taxation affects the cost of investment and its profitability, and thus the return on investment. This impact is not just a question of looking at the headline rate of tax on profits. The tax burden on the investor depends on a number of factors and their interaction, including expenses allowed, rates of capital allowances (tax depreciation), the availability of tax credits, investment allowances and tax holidays, loss carry-forward provisions, and the taxation of dividends, among other things. Together, these make up the overall fiscal regime that affects the cost of and return on investment.

Comparative tax modelling is a method of taking into account the most important of these variables in the fiscal regime in a manner that facilitates comparison between countries. The tax variables included in the analysis are:

- Corporate income tax;

- Rate of tax including tax holidays, if any;

- Loss carry-forward provisions;

- Capital allowances, investment allowances and investment credits; and

- Tax on dividends.

VAT, sales tax and import duties are not considered in this analysis.

Financial models of project investment and financing, revenues and expenses are utilized for a hypothetical business in each sector. These are based on typical costs and revenues experienced in such businesses in a developing economy. The business models cover a selected business within each sector.

The fiscal regime in El Salvador and the chosen comparator countries for each sector are applied to the standard business model for each sector over 10 years, beginning with the initial investment. The financial models calculate net cash flow to the investor, assuming that the company pays out all residual profits after tax (100 per cent dividend payout) and that the investor gains the residual value of the company, which is sold after 10 years for an amount equal to its balance sheet value.

The impact of the fiscal regime is presented as the present value of tax (PV tax per cent). PV tax per cent is the total of taxes collected by the Government over the 10 years as a percentage of the project cash flow pre-tax and post-finance, where both cash flows are discounted to a present value at a rate of 10 per cent per annum. PV tax per cent thus measures how much of an investor's potential project return is taken by the Government in taxes and duties. The higher the PV tax per cent, the more the fiscal regime burdens investors and reduces the incentive to invest.

SELECTED REFERENCES

Creskoff S and Walkenhorst P (2009). Implications of WTO disciplines for special economic zones in developing countries. World Bank policy research working paper no. 4892. Washington D.C.

Dirección General de Aduanas and USAID (2008). *Guía Aduanera*. San Salvador.

Eaton S and Shepherd AW (2001). Contract farming. Partnership for growth. FAO Agricultural Services Bulletin 145. Rome.

International Finance Corporation (2009). *Doing Business 2010. El Salvador*. Washington D.C.

Madani D (1999). A review of the role and impact of export processing zones. World Bank policy research working paper no. 2238. Washington D.C.

OECD (2008). *El Salvador: Peer Review of Competition Law and Policy*. Paris.

Saca NS and Caceres LR (2006). What do remittances do? Analysing the private remittance transmission mechanism in El Salvador. IMF working paper 06/250. Washington D.C.

UNCTAD (2001). *World Investment Report: Promoting Linkages*. United Nations publication. Sales no. E.01. II.D.12. New York and Geneva.

UNCTAD (2007). *Aftercare: A Core Function in Investment Promotion*. United Nations publication. UNCTAD/ ITE/IPC/2007/1. New York and Geneva.

UNCTAD (2008). *Investment Promotion Agencies as Policy Advocates*. United Nations publication. UNCTAD/ ITE/IPC/2007/6. New York and Geneva.

UNCTAD (2009a). *Best Practices in Investment for Development. How to Utilize FDI to Improve Infrastructure – Electricity*. United Nations publication. New York and Geneva.

UNCTAD (2009b). *Best Practices in Investment for Development. How to Utilize FDI to Improve Transport Infrastructure – Roads*. United Nations publication. New York and Geneva.

UNCTAD (2009c). *Promoting Investment and Trade: Practices and Issues*. United Nations publication. UNCTAD/ DIAE/PCB/2009/9. New York and Geneva.

UNCTAD (2009d). *The Role of International Investment Agreements in Attracting Foreign Direct Investment to Developing Countries*. United Nations publication. Sales no. E.09.II.D.20. New York and Geneva.

UNCTAD (2009e). *UNCTAD Training Manual on Statistics for FDI and the Operations of TNCs. Volume I: FDI Flows and Stock Data*. United Nations publication. E.09.II.D.2. New York and Geneva.

UNCTAD (2009f). *UNCTAD Training Manual on Statistics for FDI and the Operations of TNCs. Volume II: Statistics on the Operations of Transnational Corporations*. United Nations publication. Sales no. E.09.II.D.6. New York and Geneva.

UNCTAD (2009g). *UNCTAD Training Manual on Statistics for FDI and the Operations of TNCs. Volume III: Collecting and Reporting FDI/TNC Statistics: Institutional Issues*. United Nations publication. E.09.II.D.17. New York and Geneva.

UNCTAD (2009h). *World Investment Report 2009: Transnational Corporations, Agricultural Production and Development.* United Nations publication. E.09.II.D.15. New York and Geneva.

UNCTAD (forthcoming, a). *Best Practices in Investment for Development. How to Attract and Benefit from FDI in Small Countries.* United Nations publication. New York and Geneva.

UNCTAD (forthcoming, b). *Best Practices in Investment for Development. How to Create and Benefit from Foreign Affiliate–Domestic SME Linkages.* United Nations publication. New York and Geneva.

UNCTAD (forthcoming, c). *Best Practices in Investment for Development. How to Integrate FDI in the Skills Development Process.* United Nations publication. New York and Geneva.

UNCTAD (forthcoming, d). *Exploring Alternatives to Investment Treaty Arbitration and the Prevention of Investor–State Disputes.* United Nations publication. New York and Geneva.

UNCTAD (forthcoming, e). *International Investment Agreements. Scope and Definitions.* United Nations publication. New York and Geneva..

World Bank (2007). *República de El Salvador. Análisis Ambiental de País. Mejorando la Gestión Ambiental para Abordar la Liberalización Comercial y la Expansión de Infraestructura.* Washington D.C.

World Bank (2008). *Special Economic Zones. Performance, Lessons Learned, and Implications for Zone Development.* Washington D.C.

World Customs Organization (2004). *Customs International Benchmarking. Benchmarking Manual.* Brussels.

World Customs Organization (2008). *Customs in the 21st Century. Enhancing Growth and Development through Trade Facilitation and Border Security.* Brussels.

SELECTED UNCTAD PUBLICATIONS ON TNCS AND FDI

A.   Serial publications

World Investment Reports

http://www.unctad.org/wir

UNCTAD (2009). *World Investment Report 2009. Transnational Corporations, Agricultural Production and Development*. 280 pages. United Nations publication. Sales no. E.09.II.D.15. New York and Geneva.

UNCTAD (2008). *World Investment Report 2008. Transnational Corporations and the Infrastructure Challenge*. 294 pages. United Nations publication. Sales no. E.08.II.D.23. New York and Geneva.

UNCTAD (2007). *World Investment Report 2007. Transnational Corporations, Extractive Industries and Development*. 294 pages. United Nations publication. Sales no. E.07.II.D.9. New York and Geneva.

UNCTAD (2006). *World Investment Report 2006. FDI from Developing and Transition Economies: Implications for Development*. 340 pages. United Nations publication. Sales no. E.06.II.D.11. New York and Geneva.

UNCTAD (2005). *World Investment Report 2005. Transnational Corporations and the Internationalization of R&D*. 332 pages. United Nations publication. Sales no. E.05.II.D.10. New York and Geneva.

UNCTAD (2004). *World Investment Report 2004. The Shift Towards Services*. 468 pages. United Nations publication. Sales no. E.04.II.D.36. New York and Geneva.

UNCTAD (2003). *World Investment Report 2003. FDI Policies for Development: National and International Perspectives*. 303 pages. United Nations publication. Sales no. E.03.II.D.8. New York and Geneva.

UNCTAD (2002). *World Investment Report 2002: Transnational Corporations and Export Competitiveness*. 350 pages. United Nations publication. Sales no. E.02.II.D.4. New York and Geneva.

UNCTAD (2001). *World Investment Report 2001: Promoting Linkages*. 354 pages. United Nations publication. Sales no. E.01.II.D.12. New York and Geneva.

UNCTAD (2000). *World Investment Report 2000: Cross-border Mergers and Acquisitions and Development*. 337 pages. United Nations publication. Sales no. E.00.II.D.20. New York and Geneva.

Investment Policy Reviews

http://www.unctad.org/ipr

UNCTAD (2010). *Investment Policy Review of Sierra Leone*. 114 pages. United Nations publication. UNCTAD/DIAE/PCB/2009/14. New York and Geneva.

UNCTAD (2010). *Examen de la politique de l'investissement du Burundi*. 118 pages. United Nations publication. UNCTAD/DIAE/PCB/2009/17. New York and Geneva.

UNCTAD (2009). *Investment Policy Review of Belarus*. 111 pages. United Nations publication. UNCTAD/DIAE/PCB/2009/10. New York and Geneva.

UNCTAD (2009). *Examen de la politique de l'investissement du Burkina Faso.* 120 pages. United Nations publication. UNCTAD/DIAE/PCB/2009/4. New York and Geneva.

UNCTAD (2008). *Examen de la politique de l'investissement de la Mauritanie.* 120 pages. United Nations publication. UNCTAD/ITE/IPC/2008/5. New York and Geneva.

UNCTAD (2009). *Investment Policy Review of Nigeria.* 140 pages. United Nations publication. UNCTAD/DIAE/PCB/2008/1. New York and Geneva.

UNCTAD (2008). *Investment Policy Review of the Dominican Republic.* 116 pages. United Nations publication. UNCTAD/ITE/IPC/2007/9. New York and Geneva.

UNCTAD (2008). *Investment Policy Review of Viet Nam.* 158 pages. United Nations publication. UNCTAD/ITE/IPC/2007/10. New York and Geneva.

UNCTAD (2009). *Examen de la politique de l'investissement du Maroc.* 142 pages. United Nations publication. UNCTAD/ITE/IPC/2006/16. New York and Geneva.

UNCTAD (2007). *Report on the Implementation of the Investment Policy Review of Uganda.* 30 pages. United Nations publication. UNCTAD/ITE/IPC/2006/15. New York and Geneva.

UNCTAD (2006). *Investment Policy Review of Zambia.* 76 pages. United Nations publication. UNCTAD/ITE/IPC/2006/14. New York and Geneva.

UNCTAD (2006). *Investment Policy Review of Rwanda.* 136 pages. United Nations publication. UNCTAD/ITE/IPC/2006/11. New York and Geneva.

UNCTAD (2006). *Investment Policy Review of Colombia.* 86 pages. United Nations publication. UNCTAD/ITE/IPC/2005/11. New York and Geneva.

UNCTAD (2005). *Report on the Implementation of the Investment Policy Review of Egypt.* 18 pages. United Nations publication. UNCTAD/ITE/IPC/2005/7. New York and Geneva.

UNCTAD (2005). *Investment Policy Review of Kenya.* 114 pages. United Nations publication. UNCTAD/ITE/IPC/2005/8. New York and Geneva.

UNCTAD (2005). *Examen de la politique de l'investissement du Bénin.* 126 pages. United Nations publication. UNCTAD/ITE/IPC/2004/4. New York and Geneva.

UNCTAD (2004). *Examen de la politique de l'investissement de l'Algérie.* 110 pages. United Nations publication. UNCTAD/ITE/IPC/2003/9. New York and Geneva.

UNCTAD (2003). *Investment Policy Review of Sri Lanka.* 89 pages. United Nations publication. UNCTAD/ITE/IPC/2003/8. New York and Geneva.

UNCTAD (2003). *Investment Policy Review of Lesotho.* 105 pages. United Nations publication. Sales no. E.03.II.D.18. New York and Geneva.

UNCTAD (2003). *Investment Policy Review of Nepal.* 89 pages. United Nations publication. Sales no. E.03.II.D.17. New York and Geneva.

UNCTAD (2002). *Investment Policy Review of Ghana*. 103 pages. United Nations publication. Sales no. E.02. II.D.20. New York and Geneva.

UNCTAD (2003). *Investment Policy Review of Botswana*. 107 pages. United Nations publication. Sales no. E.03. II.D.1. New York and Geneva.

UNCTAD (2002). *Investment Policy Review: the United Republic of Tanzania*. 109 pages. United Nations publication. Sales no. E.02.II.D.6. New York and Geneva.

UNCTAD (2001). *Investment and Innovation Policy Review of Ethiopia*. 130 pages. United Nations publication. Sales no. E.01.II.D.5. New York and Geneva.

UNCTAD (2001). *Investment Policy Review of Ecuador*. 136 pages. United Nations publication. Sales no. E.01. II.D.31. New York and Geneva. Also available in Spanish.

UNCTAD (2000). *Investment Policy Review of Mauritius*. 92 pages. United Nations publication. Sales no. E.00. II.D.11. New York and Geneva.

UNCTAD (2000). *Investment Policy Review of Peru*. 109 pages. United Nations publication. Sales no. E.00. II.D.7. New York and Geneva.

UNCTAD (1999). *Investment Policy Review of Uganda*. 71 pages. United Nations publication. Sales no. E.99. II.D.24. New York and Geneva.

UNCTAD (1999). *Investment Policy Review of Uzbekistan*. 65 pages. United Nations publication. UNCTAD/ITE/IIP/Misc.13. New York and Geneva.

UNCTAD (1999). *Investment Policy Review of Egypt*. 119 pages. United Nations publication. Sales no. E.99. II.D.20. New York and Geneva.

Blue Books on Best Practice in Investment Promotion and Facilitation

UNCTAD (2005). *Blue Book on Best Practice in Investment Promotion and Facilitation: Kenya*. United Nations publication. New York and Geneva.

UNCTAD (2005). *Blue Book on Best Practice in Investment Promotion and Facilitation: United Republic of Tanzania*. United Nations publication. New York and Geneva.

UNCTAD (2005). *Blue Book on Best Practice in Investment Promotion and Facilitation: Uganda*. United Nations publication. New York and Geneva.

UNCTAD (2004). *Blue Book on Best Practice in Investment Promotion and Facilitation: Cambodia*. United Nations publication. New York and Geneva.

UNCTAD (2004). *Blue Book on Best Practice in Investment Promotion and Facilitation: Lao People's Democratic Republic*. United Nations publication. New York and Geneva.

Investment Guides

http://www.unctad.org/investmentguides

UNCTAD (2006). *An Investment Guide to Rwanda: Opportunities and Conditions.* United Nations publication. UNCTAD/ITE/IIA/2006/3. New York and Geneva.

UNCTAD (2006). *An Investment Guide to Mali: Opportunities and Conditions.* United Nations publication. UNCTAD/ITE/IIA/2006/2. New York and Geneva.

UNCTAD and ICC (2005). *An Investment Guide to East Africa.* United Nations publication. UNCTAD/IIA/2005/4. New York and Geneva.

UNCTAD and ICC (2005). *An Investment Guide to Tanzania.* United Nations publication. UNCTAD/IIA/2005/3. New York and Geneva. Free of charge.

UNCTAD and ICC (2005). *An Investment Guide to Kenya.* United Nations publication. UNCTAD/IIA/2005/2. New York and Geneva.

UNCTAD and ICC (2004). *An Investment Guide to Mauritania.* United Nations publication. UNCTAD/IIA/2004/4. New York and Geneva.

UNCTAD and ICC (2003). *An Investment Guide to Cambodia.* United Nations publication. UNCTAD/IIA/2003/6. New York and Geneva.

UNCTAD and ICC (2003). *An Investment Guide to Nepal.* United Nations publication. UNCTAD/IIA/2003/2. New York and Geneva.

UNCTAD and ICC (2002). *An Investment Guide to Mozambique.* United Nations publication. UNCTAD/IIA/4. New York and Geneva.

UNCTAD and ICC (2001). *An Investment Guide to Uganda.* United Nations publication. Symbol: UNCTAD/ITE/IIT/Misc.30. Publication updated in 2004. New symbol: UNCTAD/ITE/IIA/2004/3. New York and Geneva.

UNCTAD and ICC (2001). *An Investment Guide to Mali.* United Nations publication. Symbol: UNCTAD/ITE/IIT/Misc.24. Publication updated in 2004. New symbol: UNCTAD/ITE/IIA/2004/1. New York and Geneva.

UNCTAD and ICC (2000). *An Investment Guide to Ethiopia.* United Nations publication. Symbol: UNCTAD/ITE/IIT/Misc.19. Publication updated in 2004. New symbol: UNCTAD/ITE/IIA/2004/2. New York and Geneva.

UNCTAD and ICC (2000). *An Investment Guide to Bangladesh.* United Nations publication. UNCTAD/ITE/IIT/Misc.29. New York and Geneva.

Issues in International Investment Agreements

http://www.unctad.org/iia

UNCTAD (2006). *Bilateral Investment Treaties 1995–2006: Trends in Investment Rulemaking.* United Nations publication. New York and Geneva.

UNCTAD (2006). *Investment Provisions in Economic Integration Agreements.* United Nations publication. New York and Geneva.

UNCTAD (2003). *Glossary of Key Concepts Used in IIAs.* UNCTAD series on issues in international investment agreements. United Nations publication. New York and Geneva.

UNCTAD (2003). *Incentives.* UNCTAD series on issues in international investment agreements. United Nations publication. Sales no. E.04.II.D.6. New York and Geneva.

UNCTAD (2003). *Transparency.* UNCTAD series on issues in international investment agreements. United Nations publication. Sales no. E.03.II.D.7. New York and Geneva.

UNCTAD (2003). *Dispute Settlement: Investor–State.* UNCTAD series on issues in international investment agreements. United Nations publication. Sales no. E.03.II.D.5. New York and Geneva.

UNCTAD (2003). *Dispute Settlement: State–State.* UNCTAD series on issues in international investment agreements. United Nations publication. Sales no. E.03.II.D.6. New York and Geneva.

UNCTAD (2001). *Transfer of Technology.* UNCTAD series on issues on international investment agreements. United Nations publication. Sales no. E.01.II.D.33. New York and Geneva.

UNCTAD (2001). *Illicit Payments.* UNCTAD series on issues on international investment agreements. United Nations publication. Sales no. E.01.II.D.20. New York and Geneva.

UNCTAD (2001). *Home Country Measures.* UNCTAD series on issues on international investment agreements. United Nations publication. Sales no. E.01.II.D.19. New York and Geneva.

UNCTAD (2001). *Host Country Operational Measures.* UNCTAD series on issues on international investment agreements. United Nations publication. Sales no. E.01.II.D.18. New York and Geneva.

UNCTAD (2001). *Social Responsibility.* UNCTAD series on issues on international investment agreements. United Nations publication. Sales no. E.01.II.D.4. New York and Geneva.

UNCTAD (2001). *Environment.* UNCTAD series on issues on international investment agreements. United Nations publication. Sales no. E.01.II.D.3. New York and Geneva.

UNCTAD (2000). *Transfer of Funds.* UNCTAD series on issues on international investment agreements. United Nations publication. Sales no. E.00.II.D.38. New York and Geneva.

UNCTAD (2000). *Flexibility for Development.* UNCTAD series on issues on international investment agreements. United Nations publication. Sales no. E.00.II.D.6. New York and Geneva.

UNCTAD (2000). *Employment.* UNCTAD series on issues on international investment agreements. United Nations publication. Sales no. E.00.II.D.15. New York and Geneva.

UNCTAD (2000). *Taxation.* UNCTAD series on issues on international investment agreements. United Nations publication. Sales no. E.00.II.D.5. New York and Geneva.

UNCTAD (2000). *Taking of Property.* UNCTAD series on issues on international investment agreements. United Nations publication. Sales no. E.00.II.D.4. New York and Geneva.

International Investment Instruments

UNCTAD (2000). *UNCTAD's Work Programme on International Investment Agreements: From UNCTAD IX to UNCTAD X*. United Nations publication. UNCTAD/ITE/IIT/Misc.26. New York and Geneva. Available free of charge.

UNCTAD (2002). *Progress Report. Work undertaken within UNCTAD's work programme on international investment agreements between the 10th Conference of UNCTAD, Bangkok, February 2000, and July 2002.* United Nations publication. UNCTAD/ITE/Misc.58. New York and Geneva. Available free of charge.

UNCTAD (1998). *Bilateral Investment Treaties in the Mid-1990s.* 322 pages. United Nations publication. Sales no. E.98.II.D.8. New York and Geneva. $46.

UNCTAD (2000). *Bilateral Investment Treaties: 1959–1999.* United Nations publication. Sales no. E.92.II.A.16. New York and Geneva. $22.

UNCTAD (1996 to 2003). *International Investment Instruments: A Compendium.* 12 volumes. Vol. I: Sales no. E.96.A.II.A.9. Vol. II: Sales no. E.96.II.A.10. Vol. III: Sales no. E.96.II.A.11. Vol. IV: Sales no. E.00.II.D.13. Vol. V: Sales no. E.00.II.A.14. Vol. VI: Sales no. E.01.II.D.34. Vol. VII: Sales no. E.02.II.D.14. Vol. VIII: Sales no. E.02.II.D.15. Vol. IX: Sales no. E.02.II.D.16. Vol. X: Sales no. E.02.II.D.21. Vol. XI: Sales no. E.04.II.D.9. Vol. XII: Sales no. E.04.II.D.10. New York and Geneva. $60.

ASIT Advisory Studies

http://www.unctad.org/asit

UNCTAD (2007). *Aftercare: A Core Function in Investment Promotion.* United Nations publication. UNCTAD/ITE/IPC/2007/1. New York and Geneva.

UNCTAD (2001). No. 17. *The World of Investment Promotion at a Glance: A Survey of Investment Promotion Practices.* United Nations publication. UNCTAD/ITE/IPC/3. New York and Geneva. Free of charge.

UNCTAD (2000). No. 16. *Tax Incentives and Foreign Direct Investment: A Global Survey.* 180 pages. United Nations publication. Sales no. E.01.II.D.5. New York and Geneva.

UNCTAD (2000). No. 15. *Investment Regimes in the Arab World: Issues and Policies.* 232 pages. United Nations publication. Sales no. E/F.00.II.D.32. New York and Geneva.

UNCTAD (1999). No. 14. *Handbook on Outward Investment Promotion Agencies and Institutions.* 50 pages. United Nations publication. Sales no. E.99.II.D.22. New York and Geneva.

UNCTAD (1997). No. 13. *Survey of Best Practices in Investment Promotion.* 71 pages. United Nations publication. Sales no. E.97.II.D.11. New York and Geneva.

B.   Individual studies

uNCTAD (2003). *Investment and Technology Policies for Competitiveness: Review of Successful Country Experiences.* United Nations publication. UNCTAD/ITE/ICP/2003/2. New York and Geneva.

UNCTAD (2003). *The Development Dimension of FDI: Policy and Rule-Making Perspectives.* United Nations publication. Sales no. E.03.II.D.22. New York and Geneva. $35.

UNCTAD (2003). *FDI and Performance Requirements: New Evidence from Selected Countries.* 318 pages. United Nations publication. Sales no. E.03.II.D.32. New York and Geneva. $35.

UNCTAD (2001). *Measures of the Transnationalization of Economic Activity.* United Nations publication. Sales no. E.01.II.D.2. New York and Geneva.

UNCTAD (2000). *FDI Determinants and TNC Strategies: The Case of Brazil.* United Nations publication. Sales no. E.00.II.D.2. New York and Geneva.

UNCTAD (2000). *The Competitiveness Challenge: Transnational Corporations and Industrial Restructuring in Developing Countries.* United Nations publication. Sales no. E.00.II.D.35. New York and Geneva.

UNCTAD (1999). *Foreign Direct Investment in Africa: Performance and Potential.* United Nations publication. UNCTAD/ITE/IIT/Misc.15. New York and Geneva. Available free of charge.

UNCTAD (1998). *The Financial Crisis in Asia and Foreign Direct Investment: An Assessment.* 110 pages. United Nations publication. Sales no. GV.E.98.0.29. New York and Geneva. $20.

UNCTAD (1998). *Handbook on Foreign Direct Investment by Small and Medium-sized Enterprises: Lessons from Asia.* 202 pages. United Nations publication. Sales no. E.98.II.D.4. New York and Geneva. $48.

UNCTAD (1998). *Handbook on Foreign Direct Investment by Small and Medium-sized Enterprises: Lessons from Asia.* Executive summary and report on the Kunming conference. 70 pages. United Nations publication. UNCTAD/ITE/IIT/6 (summary). New York and Geneva. Available free of charge.

UNCTAD (1996). *Incentives and Foreign Direct Investment.* Current Studies, series A, no. 30. 98 pages. United Nations publication. Sales no. E.96.II.A.6. New York and Geneva. $25.

UNCTAD (1996). *Foreign Direct Investment, Trade, Aid and Migration.* Current Studies, series A, no. 29. 90 pages. Joint publication of the United Nations and the International Organization for Migration, Geneva. Sales no. E.96M.A.8. New York and Geneva. $25.

UNCTAD (1993). *Explaining and Forecasting Regional Flows of Foreign Direct Investment.* Current Studies, series A, no. 26. 58 pages. United Nations publication. Sales no. E.94.II.A.5. New York and Geneva. $25.

UNCTAD (1993). *Small and Medium-sized Transnational Corporations: Role, Impact and Policy Implications.* 242 pages. United Nations publication. Sales no. E.93.II.A. 15. New York and Geneva. $35.

UNCTAD (1994). *Small and Medium-sized Transnational Corporations: Executive Summary and Report of the Osaka Conference.* 60 pages. United Nations publication. New York and Geneva. Available free of charge.

UNCTC (1988). *Foreign Direct Investment in the People's Republic of China.* 110 pages. United Nations publication. Sales no. E.88.II.A.3. New York. Out of print. Available on microfiche. Paper copy from microfiche: $122.

C.   Journals

Transnational Corporations Journal (formerly *The CTC Reporter*). Published three times a year. Annual subscription price: $45. Individual issues: $20.

READERSHIP SURVEY
Investment Policy Review of El Salvador

In order to improve the quality and relevance of the work of the UNCTAD Division on Investment and Enterprise, it would be useful to receive the views of readers on this and other similar publications. It would therefore be greatly appreciated if you could complete the following questionnaire and return it to:

Readership Survey

UNCTAD, Division on Investment and Enterprise
Palais des Nations
Room E-10074
CH-1211 Geneva 10
Switzerland
Or by Fax to: 41-22-9170197

> This questionnaire is also available to be filled out on line at:
> **www.unctad.org/ipr**

1. Name and professional address of respondent (optional):

_____

_____

2. Which of the following best describes your area of work?

Government	○	Public enterprise	○
Private enterprise institution	○	Academic or research	○
International organization	○	Media	○
Not-for-profit organization	○	Other (specify)	○

3. In which country do you work?

4. What is your assessment of the contents of this publication?

Excellent	○	Adequate	○
Good	○	Poor	○

5. How useful is this publication to your work?

Very useful ○   Of some use ○   Irrelevant ○

6. Please indicate the three things you liked best about this publication and are useful to your work:

_____

_____

_____

_____

7. Please indicate the three things you liked least about this publication:

_____

_____

_____

8. If you have read more than the present publication of the UNCTAD Division on Investment and Enterprise, what is your overall assessment of them?

Consistently good ⭕   Usually good, but with some exceptions ⭕

Generally mediocre ⭕   Poor ⭕

9. On the average, how useful are these publications to you in your work?

Very useful ⭕   Of some use ⭕   Irrelevant ⭕

10. Are you a regular recipient of Transnational Corporations (formerly The CTC Reporter), the Division's tri-annual refereed journal?

Yes ⭕   No ⭕

If not, please check here if you would like to receive a sample copy sent to the name and address you have given above. Other titles you would like to receive instead (see list of publications).

_____

_____

_____

11. How or where did you get this publication:

I bought it ⭕   In a seminar/workshop ⭕

I requested a courtesy copy ⭕   Direct mailing ⭕

Other ⭕

12. Would you like to receive information on the work of UNCTAD in the area of Investment and Enterprise through e-mail ? If yes, please write your e-mail address below:

_____

United Nations publications may be obtained from bookstores and distributors throughout the world. Please consult your bookstore, or:

For Africa and Europe, write to:

Sales Section
United Nations Office at Geneva
Palais des Nations
CH-1211 Geneva 10
Switzerland
Tel: +41 22 917 1234
Fax: +41 22 917 0123
E-mail: unpubli@unog.ch

For Asia and the Pacific, the Caribbean, Latin America and North America, write to:

Sales Section
Room DC2-0853
United Nations Secretariat
New York, NY 10017
United States
Tel: +1 212 963 8302 or 1 800 253 9646
Fax: +1 212 963 3489
E-mail: publications@un.org

All prices are quoted in United States dollars.

For further information on the work of UNCTAD's Division on Investment and Enterprise, please address your inquiries to:

United Nations Conference on Trade and Development
Division on Investment and Enterprise
Palais des Nations, Room E-10054
CH-1211 Geneva 10, Switzerland
Telephone: +41 22 917 5760
Fax: +41 22 917 0498
E-mail: natalia.meramo@unctad.org
http://www.unctad.org